Cheer Up, Mate!

Cheer Up, Mate!

SECOND WORLD WAR HUMOUR

ALAN WEEKS

The
History
Press

Cover illustration: Old Bill and Co. by Bruce Bairnsfather. (Illustrated London News Ltd/Mary Evans)

First published 2011

The History Press
The Mill, Brimscombe Port
Stroud, Gloucestershire, GL5 2QG
www.thehistorypress.co.uk

British Library Cataloguing in Publication Data.
A catalogue record for this book is available from the British
Library.

ISBN 978 0 7524 5972 1

Typesetting and origination by The History Press
Printed in Great Britain

Contents

ONE

The Bore War

'Are they here?'

The day war broke out my mother said to me, 'You can go out and play but don't be late because the German bombers might come'.

'Will they come down the 57 or the 56?' I enquired. I was about three months short of my fifth birthday. The number 57 bus came south to Cubitt Town (Isle of Dogs, East London) from Poplar and the 56 went north from Cubitt Town to Mile End, Bow.

'I don't know,' she admitted.

She needn't have worried about the German bombers: they didn't arrive for a year, not in my neck of the woods, anyway. Millions of children and their mums had been shifted out of the cities (600,000 between Friday 1 September and Sunday 3 September, 1939 alone) when war was announced. A lot of them returned home before Christmas because nothing seemed to be happening. It was 'The Bore War', later 'The Phoney War' (American terminology eventually won through here). Indeed, newspaper vendors got fed up with the lack of news and printed their own on the billboards:

Latest – Germans in Berlin. Evening Paper ... Scots in Aberdeen.

Up the road from me in Romford a terrible storm was raging after the prime minister, Neville Chamberlain, had spoken to the nation, and

Air-raid warning, 3 September 1939. (London Regional Transport)

little Alice Greer, who had heard that war was noisy, asked her mum, 'Are they here?'

Just seven minutes after the prime minister announced war the first real air-raid siren began to wail (indicating that enemy bombers were twelve minutes away – according to official instructions) and the police pedalled furiously up and down streets bearing placards which read 'TAKE COVER'. It was a false alarm.

One lady in Birmingham sympathised with Mr Chamberlain having to declare war on the Sabbath, but at least this lady and Alice had some idea that conflict had started. Donald Wheal's mum didn't tell him until the 7th. However, by then, he was probably wondering why they had all suddenly left home in Chelsea and gone to Woking.

Gas masks

The public had been warned about all sorts of gases – lung irritant, tear gas, sneezing gas, blister gas – and there were frequent panics caused by floor polish, mustard, musty hay, bleach powder, horseradish, geraniums, pear drops, etc.

Meanwhile, the BBC helpfully advised listeners not to try out their masks in turned-on gas ovens or by their car exhaust pipes. Small children had a 'Mickey Mouse' mask and soon discovered that by blowing through the rubber vent they could produce a rude noise. Infants were completely enveloped in something resembling a tent. The tops of many pillar-boxes were painted yellow with gas detector paint: when gas was around they were supposed to change colour. Special masks were designed for animals: the one for shire horses weighed a kilo (or 2.2 pounds, as they called it in those days).

People became particularly worried about their pet dogs. Mrs Parmenter of Plaistow, who boarded dogs, received a lot of enquiries about kennelling dogs during air raids. Perhaps she was known to be bombproof.

After the first air-raid warning Odette Lesley and her family frantically tried to don their new masks. Her mother's ended up round

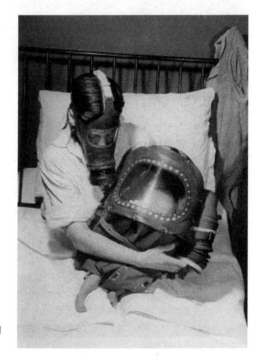

Gas masks for infants. (Reproduced by kind permission of the Trustees of the Imperial War Museum (3918))

Doggie
gas mask,
1939. (Watford
Central Library)

the back of her head, her sister's suspended from her left ear and
Odette's jammed inside her jumper.

However, a great deal of training went into the proper use of the
masks. In fact, by 19 September Kay Phipps had been awarded her
Chemical War Certificate, including the ability to respond correctly
to the instructor's vital question, 'What do you do on receiving the
warning "Gas Attack"?'.

In response, Kay and her fellow students, 'Miss Twitter' and 'Miss
Flaps', had learnt to chant: 'Attend to the wants of nature!' At which
point 'Miss Twitter' and 'Miss Flaps' collapsed into helpless giggles.

Even more assistance was forthcoming from newspapers,
especially the advertisement for Sanotogen Nerve-Tonic Food,
described as a 'national necessity for preserving good nerves in the
current situation'.

Evacuation

Operation Pied Piper moved nearly four million evacuees in 1939. The inhabitants of the village of Waltham St Lawrence in Berkshire were warned to expect hordes of these 'shadow trekkers'. It could be hard going for evacuee and host. On a train from Birkenhead heads were examined and 10-year-old Doreen was interrogated: 'Is your brother a breeder?'

Following due inspections there could be an ordeal by Dettol, grotesque bright pink or bright green disinfectants, or soft soap, paraffin or vinegar, plus a metal Derbac Comb (which hurt, I can tell you). Some nurses cut to the chase and sheared off whole heads of hair, such as 'Nitty Nora' of Pulborough, Sussex. One host in Lancashire purchased a cake of sheep dip from the local chemist shop.

Evacuation could also be hazardous: tiny Syd Smith, on his way to Frome by train from Paddington with his little suitcase, containing a bar of Fry's Chocolate, an apple, a *Tin Can Tommy* comic and spare shirts and braces, stuck his head out of a window and his prized cap

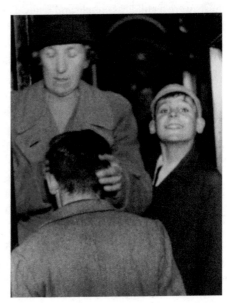

Looking for hair nits during evacuation, 1939. (Reproduced by kind permission of the Trustees of the Imperial War Museum (D595))

flew off in the breeze. Syd screamed blue murder and demanded that the train be halted so that he could retrieve his beloved headgear.

Indeed, he became so excited that a Bulls Eyes boiled sweet (guaranteed to last half an hour) lodged securely between his teeth. As anxious adults shook him about a bit he caught his finger in a sliding door.

At the same time, there were also difficulties for well-meaning hosts. The dirt accumulated on the legs and neck of a small boy from Salford resisted several applications of very hot water and carbolic soap. After the operation was eventually successful he exclaimed cheerfully, 'Cor, I don't half feel funny!'

At least they managed to get him into a bath: others adamantly refused to go in a tub through fear of drowning. Laying in a bed was considered inappropriate because back at some homes this happened only to corpses. Ignorance of country ways was also widespread: milk from cows was urine in the estimation of some children from the cities.

I was evacuated and went to Long Hanborough near Oxford with my sister, who was four years older than me (she was 9 at the time). It was a hard winter and I was eventually rescued by my family. Our hosts were a childless couple and really didn't know how to look after us. The wife thought it was her duty to totally protect the well-being of her husband. During the evenings we had to stay in an unheated kitchen whilst our hosts sat round a roaring fire in the living room. I got frostbite in my feet.

Uncle Willie kindly brought my parents down in his Ford 8 (my sister had managed to smuggle a letter home). Uncle Willie was also able to trip up my father as he went to beat the hell out of the husband, and then bundle my dad back into the car. We sped off at speed whilst the wife ran to the phone box to get in touch with the constabulary.

Later in the war, my mother, older sister and I were evacuated to Nantgaredig in the wilds of Carmarthenshire. Soon after we arrived our host, an elderly and frail Mrs Jones living on her own, went down with pneumonia. My mother, in response to loud protests from cows crammed with milk, sat on a stool in a freezing barn in the dead of night delivering them from their torture.

Meanwhile, in Warrington, the discovery that there were apples hanging down from trees induced evacuee Lucy Gale to stuff some of them inside her knickers, but the elastic snapped as she was climbing the stairs and the fruit tumbled down before the gaze of her hosts (who owned the orchard).

Trying to pair evacuees with hosts in village halls created scenes like those at a Roman slave market or Selfridges' bargain basement. Potential billeters looked out for clean, sturdy-looking children and this process eventually left a residue of dirty and scrawny ones, plus sisters and brothers who refused steadfastly to be parted, the last piece of advice from mum still ringing in their ears.

Finding themselves in strange and uninviting surroundings the more literary of the evacuees fired off quick letters:

Dear Mum,
I don't like the man's face. I don't like the lady's face much. Perhaps it will look better in daylight. I like the dog's face best.

Dear Mum,
I do not like it here very much. I feel homesick. I want to come home. Hope everyone is well and happy,
Love to all
Keith.
P.S. I mean it.

Some young travellers could be assertive. An older boy from Paddington advised his two rather elegant spinster hosts in Oxford, 'I'll put meself to bed so that you two old geezers can get down the boozer.'

Indeed, the main character in the Richmal Crompton books, William, was asked by his chums to arrange their own evacuation away from the dreadful evacuees – fiction, but based on fact presumably. No wonder that some citizens, fortunately well-off, arranged to escape to faraway places. An actress who stopped at a luxury hotel in North Wales discovered ladies there who devoted their time to drinking, backgammon and knitting for the troops.

George Beardmore found himself employed in Wembley in November 1939 to try and trace householders who had made abrupt departures – without paying their rates (council tax). But knocking on neighbours' front doors proved unproductive, and unpopular. Milkmen, postmen, road sweepers and dustmen were better sources of information, but best of all was the gasman, also concerned with unpaid bills. George arranged to meet him on Saturday mornings in the Express Dairy Café and buy him a cup of tea in exchange for relevant information.

Less affluent Cockneys decided to go 'opping' (picking hops in the Kent countryside), an annual event intended to add to the family income and get a change of air. In 1939 many 'oppers' negotiated a longer sojourn than usual.

Around this time, the Coalition War Government, in its wisdom, provided a Neurosis Centre and a War Emergency Clinic for 'psychological victims' of air attacks. They were finally closed within a few months for total lack of customers. Such resilience was possibly due to Horlicks Malted Milk, which, it said on the tin, provided a 'third level of sleep' (also claimed by Sanotogen Nerve-Tonic Food).

Waste not – and other tribulations

Back in the cities parents upset at the departure of their little ones could cheer themselves up with the rumour that Adolf Hitler went round with a gun in his pocket to shoot himself if things didn't go according to his well-laid plans (he was no longer politely referred to as 'Herr Hitler'). Even more welcome was the story that two of his food-tasters had been poisoned. There was widespread support for the view that Adolf needed a long, lingering death caused by rat poison and ground glass.

Meanwhile, back in the real world, belts and braces were being tightened. 'Waste not, want not' was the order of the day, backed by rather colourful advertising boards. One favourite depicted a mob of enthusiastic housewives pelting Hitler and co. with kitchen junk, Zeppelin parts, Pickelhaube helmets and diverse *objets d'art*.

Advice flowed in from many sources: slice up your Mars bars and enjoy just one slice at a time, grow cabbages on the roof of your Anderson air-raid shelter. The head chef at the Savoy promoted 'Lord Woolton's Vegetable Pie' – potato, swede, cauliflower and carrot plus anything else left over (Lord Woolton was the Minister of Food).

There were suggestions for 'perking up' this official pie, such as 'Symington's Vita-Gravy' and 'Surprise Potato Balls'. Cynthia Gillett, evacuated from Woolwich to Edworth in Bedfordshire, remembered (not fondly) school dinners of bread spread with stewed rhubarb.

Similarly, on the BBC Home Service on 4 October, W.H. Barrington Dalby advised listeners to avoid opening their fridges (if they had one) more than 6in and to convert hot-water bottles into vacuum flasks – all in the interests of conserving energy. It was also 'patriotic' to have only 5in of water in your bath (no fear of drowning there).

The *Daily Mail* of 14 October 1939 announced the creation of the government office of 'Controller of Shirts', nonsense almost on a par with *It's That Man Again (ITMA)* and their 'Office of Twerps'. *ITMA* was the most popular radio comedy of the day, and starred Tommy Handley (or 'Mr Handpump') and favourites like the charlady 'Mrs Mopp' with her catchphrase 'Can I do you now, sir?'.

There was also 'Funf', the German spy with feet of sauerkraut. The 'Office of Twerps' was part of the 'Ministry of Aggravation and Mysteries'.

'I have the power to seize anything,' Mr Handpump informed Vera, his secretary.

'Oh, Mr Handpump!' gasped Vera, 'and me sitting so close to you.'

Another favourite on the radio and the music hall stage at this time was Rob Wilton, a comedian from the North, whose catchphrase opening I borrowed for the first sentence of this book, except that he said 'my missus' and not 'my mother'.

The Ministry of Information, it seemed, became the Ministry for Disinformation. Of course, the real ministry itself created many a laugh with its poster characters 'Miss Leaky Mouth', 'Mr Glumpot',

'Mr Secrecy Hush-Hush', 'Mr Knowall', 'Miss Teacup Whisper' and 'Mr Pride in Prophecy'.

Given all these trials and tribulations, the government was keen on testing the morale of the people. The Ministry of Information set up a Home Intelligence Department in Senate House in London to test the state of the nation's nerves. This had an enormous network of observers – bus and train inspectors, W.H. Smith managers, cinema supervisors, Citizens' Advice Bureau staff, trade union officials, council officials, social workers and Mass Observation (M.O.) diarists.

M.O. was founded by Tom Harrisson and Charles Madge in 1937. Hundreds of ordinary people volunteered to attempt to write and submit a daily diary of their lives and those of the folk they knew. It is a rich source of social history, now kept in archives at the University of Sussex.

Blackout

The blackout on windows and street lighting was a further trial of nerves. Woe betide the householder who showed the merest chink of light: not only were you at the mercy of wily patrolling Air-raid Precaution (ARP) Wardens but also, in more select neighbourhoods, 'Soroptimist Clubs', perambulating groups of middle-aged, middle-class lady vigilantes. If they found you out it was a case of serving them tea and biscuits and conversation. The ARP might be preferable. It was a matter of conviction that a Dornier pilot could see you light a fag from 20,000ft.

Moving around at night was thus an ordeal. One estimate was that 20 per cent of the population was injured in the dark during the course of the war. Road accidents rose alarmingly; one woman collided with an elephant on its way to a circus venue. Even the buses just had dull sidelights and no inner illumination. Mrs Jane Steward dropped a bag of cakes on a bus in Bromley on 21 October: the conductor fell over a jam tart and all hell was let loose.

Meanwhile the ARP had to keep on their toes despite the lack of real action – which, to numerous critics, was no more than grown men playing games in the street. Unenthusiastic volunteers were

Luminous gadgets to prevent road accidents during the blackout. They were not popular, as the slashed prices indicate. (Reproduced by kind permission of the Trustees of the Imperial War Museum (D78))

pressed into service. One 'casualty' left a note: 'Have bled to death and gone home.'

Come Halloween, Nella Last's husband was determined to celebrate. Nella was one of the Mass Observationists, living in Barrow-in-Furness. Duly, on 31 October, he decorated his front door with elaborate and sinister designs adorned with the message 'Abandon hope all ye who enter here'. Combined with the pitch-darkness of the house and street it was quite effective.

Air-raid warnings

Despite the lack of serious bombing in 1939 there were plenty of air-raid warnings; a siren rather like hundreds of vuvuzelas creating an undulating racket. The 'All-Clear' was at least on one note and it was a relief to hear it. There was such a warning in Barking on 6 October and elderly Edith Sims called to her husband:

'What's to do, Joe?'

'Jerry's over!' Joe called back.

'Never mind, Joe, have a cup of tea, mate,' Edith consoled him. 'You can mop it up in the morning.'

(A 'Jerry' was a bedroom chamber pot, or 'po', as well as a German. This drama was reported in the *Berlin Liar*, a publication dedicated to repudiating anything Lord Haw-Haw said.)

In the air

Meanwhile, Hitler was destroying Poland and the Russians were trying, unsuccessfully, to do the same to Finland. We supported the Finns but later in the war we supported the Soviet Union against the Nazis. The Royal Air Force (RAF) was trying to do its bit and was frequently over the Fatherland bombing the civilian population – with propaganda leaflets, which led to the story (possibly someone's idea of a joke) of the air crew who jettisoned untied and heavy bundles of leaflets on defenceless civilians. On debriefing they were severely reprimanded by the wing commander; someone might have been hurt.

It was suggested to the Secretary for Air – Sir Kingsley Wood – that bombers could set fire to the Black Forest. He was horrified at the idea: 'Are you aware that the Black Forest is private property?' he demanded. 'Why, you will be asking me to bomb Essen next!'

There is a similar tale about Spike Milligan's uncle. He wanted to drop hundreds of wooden mushrooms (made by him in his shed) on the German populace in order to convince them that British craftsmanship was as good as ever. He was turned down by the Air Ministry, on the grounds that they had no desire to injure innocent Germans. A British cartoon of 6 September showed Hitler on his knees begging us to rain famine, bombs and gas onto these innocent Germans, but not the truth.

There was some real action in the air, however: some Junkers 88s attacked battleships at Rosyth on the north side of the Firth of Forth on 16 October. Four of the bombers were shot down by pilots of the Auxiliary Air Force.

'Saturday Afternoon Airmen shoot down Nazi Bombers' was the headline in the *Daily Express* the following morning.

The winter of 1939/40 was bitterly cold. Pilots sat around waiting for more action in freezing huts at Drem airfield in Scotland ('the coldest spot on earth') with only lukewarm stoves to thaw them out. They played 'uckers' (ludo). At least they could undo the top button of their tunics to indicate to impressionable young women that they were real pilots, and look forward to games of a different sort.

Later, in June 1940, the Luftwaffe dropped postcards on innocent civilians in Paris showing French soldiers attacking barbed-wire defences. Written across the picture was the caption, 'Where are the Tommies?'. If the Parisians held the card up to the light they could also see British officers making indecent advances towards young French girls.

The British Expeditionary Force (BEF)

The BEF returned to France, previously vacated by its predecessor in 1918 in 'the war to end all wars'. The 6th Battalion of the Durham Light Infantry was part of it. Private Thomas Russ' pal was assiduously learning French in order to make himself understood abroad. As soon as he stepped foot in the county his first words were, 'Where's the NAAFI, mate?'

The dangers which confronted Tommies in 1914–18 were still in evidence. Young Wilfred Saunders joined a queue for 'Fish and Chips' only to discover that it was for a brothel. He ran off quickly before someone asked him for a donation.

Further north, in Flanders, Lance-Corporal Tony Bond, smothered in kisses and hugs from nice local girls, found time to send home a postcard telling his parents that 'he was having a terrible time' in the rain and mud.

William Campion of the 59 Medium Regiment, Royal Artillery, also visited a 'maison de tolérance' in Lille and claimed, in another card sent to home, that all he did was a spot of 'intimate dancing'.

At home, meanwhile, we could do our bit for the military presence. I pleaded with my dad for the latest toy (resplendent in Hamleys' display windows) – 'Build Your Own Maginot Line'.

On the real Maginot Line Captain Anthony Rhodes saw his first German soldier. A major also spotted him:

'Look, there's a German,' he exclaimed in some excitement. 'Shoot him!'

'I wouldn't, sir,' advised Captain Rhodes. 'They might shoot back.' It was early days.

RAF Fighter Command was also represented in France and carried out lots of patrols looking for the Luftwaffe. Pilot Officer Roland Beaumont, 87 Squadron, was also in Lille. However, the 'airstrip' being used by 87 was just a field and it hadn't stopped raining since the Great War. As the terrain turned into a swamp the squadron decided to fly off to look for dry ground, but the only way to get airborne was to drive up the road. Beaumont successfully managed this and flew to Le Touquet, where he was sent to the local hospital suffering from pleurisy.

Flight Sergeant G.C. Unwin remembered Douglas Bader and his tin legs in 222 Squadron. Early in 1940 Bader crashed a Spitfire into a wall and mangled them. He was sent replacements and he spent many a night scraping and scratching them to get a perfect fit. Unwin, trying to get some sleep, politely complained. *Snow White and the Seven Dwarfs* was still all the rage at the local cinema and so Bader re-christened Unwin (politely) as 'Grumpy'.

One of Grumpy's tasks was to take charge of Bader's left tin leg whilst Pilot Officer Tom Vigors looked after the right one. When the alarm went off it was their responsibility to screw the legs on.

'Cobber' Kain shot down a Messerschmitt 109 over Saarbrucken on 2 March 1940. Not long after he was drafted back to England to lecture trainee pilots on dogfight evasion.

'It's always one raider,' he explained. 'They haven't got many planes and they're also short of fuel.'

One of the trainees listening, Christopher Foxley-Ninns, was soon in the air over France and, having been alerted by the 'Arse-End Charlie' (squadron look-out), was chased around a church steeple by six Messerschmitt 109s.

Squadron Leader Roger Bushell was a pre-war barrister and famously flew up north to defend a ground crew member, changing into wig and gown and winning the case hands down. Commanding

92 Squadron on patrol he was shot down over Dunkirk (where Allied troops were rapidly heading – see the next chapter) on 23 May 1940 and captured. In March 1944 the Gestapo murdered him during the aftermath of the 'Great Escape' from Stalag Luft III.

At sea

Doreen Spencer reported for WREN (Women's Royal Naval Service) training in Portsmouth and was sharply accosted by a warrant officer.

'Why aren't you wearing your raincoat?' she demanded fiercely.

'It ain't raining,' replied Doreen, who was a straightforward soul.

'It's the regulation of the day!' screamed the warrant officer. 'And why aren't you running? Everyone runs on the quarter-deck!'

'What quarter-deck?' protested Doreen, yet to discover naval discipline. 'It's the pavement.'

'It's the bloody quarter-deck!' screeched a thoroughly worked-up warrant officer.

Doreen couldn't even boil an egg so was button-holed for culinary duties, reporting to a freezing 'galley' at 6 a.m. to peel dozens of buckets of spuds and carrots. Later in the war, promoted to telephone operator, Doreen had a call.

'Who's that?' she enquired.

'Ike.'

'Oh, yes,' scoffed Doreen. 'And I'm Mickey Mouse.'

But it actually was General Eisenhower on the other end of the line.

Doreen eventually became engaged to a sailor but he was killed in the Mediterranean. Then she became betrothed to a petty officer but he lost his life in the Atlantic. She didn't have a lot to laugh about.

It was certainly a culture shock for girls from posh backgrounds to be thrown in with ladies from more earthly environments. For instance, to the innocent (but educated) 'on the game' referred to high-level army intelligence on the North-West Frontier of the empire in India.

New Yorker James Goodson, a trained pilot, survived the sinking of the liner *Athenia* in the mid-Atlantic and, as soon as he made land, reported to the RAF recruiting office in Glasgow. Could he, as an American, join up?

'Yeah,' was the answer. 'Seven shillings and sixpence a day.'

'I'm sorry,' explained Goodson, 'I lost everything on the boat so I can't pay yet.'

'Pay?' echoed an incredulous flight sergeant. 'No, we pay you – seven and six a day.'

So James Goodson became a very happy man; allowed to fly a Spitfire and get paid for it into the bargain.

Rationing

New Year's Day's news for 1940 was that some food was to be rationed. Better news was that adolescent boys aged between 13 and 18 were to get an 'arduous supplement' – in fact, extra meat.

Workers in heavy industry would get the same treat. But further bad news was that, in the event, neither the lads nor the workers ever got any extra meat. German submarines made sure there wasn't any.

Bombed-out civilians and service personnel on leave were placed in the same category for rations – a masterpiece of bureaucracy.

Yet shortages inspired creativity: Ethel Robinson's husband, a docker in Liverpool, tried to slip past a policeman at the dock gates with a couple of nicked frozen pig hearts in an empty gas mask.

'What you got there?' demanded the copper.

'Me gas mask – what do you bloody think it is, eh?' retorted Mr Robinson.

'Well, its nose is bleeding.'

News from Glasgow

Pam Ashford in Glasgow was another M.O. diarist. Early in 1940 her work colleagues, Miss Smith and Miss Bousie, conducted a discussion about service personnel on leave in the city. Miss Bousie suggested that they looked too serious. But Miss Smith was of the opinion that they wouldn't be much good if they were not serious.

Miss Bousie was not to be denied, however, and further complained that some of these 'serious' sailors, soldiers and airmen were wearing fur coats. Since it was snowing in Corunna for the first time since 1800 Miss Smith explained that service personnel had been advised to keep warm: it was also well below zero in Glasgow so wearing fur coats seemed to be eminently sensible.

But Miss Bousie was persistent. 'Well, what about if a bomb fell on them? They would catch fire and go up in smoke. What would that do for the war effort?'

'No,' insisted Miss Smith, 'at worst they would only get singed.'

Perhaps these fur-clad soldiers and sailors had just returned from trying to secure a foothold in Norway, where it was even colder than in Glasgow. Here, General Sir Adrian Carton de Wiart, commander of the Central Norwegian Expeditionary Force, was surveying his men in the village of Harstaad. On 14 April, he noted, they were smothered in coats and socks and enormous boots and looked like 'paralysed polar bears'.

Pam Ashford continued to entertain M.O. staff in London with her almost daily contributions. Her office in Glasgow was opposite the zoo. On 24 January Mr Mitchell, her boss, believed that the lions would have to be shot in the event of an air raid. Miss Ashford mused over the tricky problem. It was hard lines on the lions, but ...

Miss Bousie also continued to make her views known. There was a solid rumour that the Germans were about to send over balloons filled with poison gas. She insisted that it was her patriotic duty, if she found one of these contraptions, to steadfastly stand by it until such time as a policeman came by, and to warn other passers-by of the danger.

Fear of air raids was widespread in the city. A friend of Pam Ashford's, an elderly lady living alone, was concerned that her dog would catch fire in the event of an attack and had prepared a large, soaking wet flannel to wrap around the mongrel, plus a tea cosy to put on his head (it stopped him barking).

Pam worked for the Forth of Clyde Coal Company. A letter she penned on 11 June was in response to an esteemed order from the Alps:

'In view of the present state of affairs in Europe we regret it will be impossible to suggest any route by which we could deliver a cargo of coal to Switzerland.'

Ways to win the war

Hector Bolitho, at the Air Ministry, was receiving many ideas from the public about how the war could be won, such as dropping lots of bombs down Mount Vesuvius and exploding southern Italy, or designing special aeroplanes which could pretend to run away from enemy aircraft and then squirt chloroform and narcotics from a rear vent to incapacitate pursuing pilots.

Another was to drop 'sticky bombs' in front of the Wehrmacht in order to halt the blitzkrieg – or coils of barbed wire. Obsolete British fighter planes (of which there were many) could fly past parachuting Luftwaffe pilots and cut their cords.

Millions of snakes could be shipped over from South Africa and dropped (on dark nights) over German cities, or even thousands of poisoned cabbage leaves on enemy cows, pigs and sheep.

The correspondent who sent the snakes idea actually lived in South Africa, in Durban. He added a footnote to the effect that the war would finish at 2.30 p.m. on 4 May 1945, with Britain as the winner.

Life goes on

Meanwhile, I had become 5 years old and started to sing silly songs:

Underneath the spreading chestnut tree
Hitler dropped a bomb on me,
Now I'm a blinking refugee.

Thousands of enormous barrage balloons floated over my head like silver elephants waiting for Hermann Goering, they didn't have long to wait. British social life went on: John White toured with his troupe of dancing girls, trying to entice customers through a loud hailer.

'Margot will now demonstrate her fan dance. What you see keep to yourself and tell nobody. If you don't see what you want to see let me know and I will see what I can do for you.'

The audience consisted mainly of plain-clothes policemen on the lookout for any affront to public decency. In fact, there had been a top-level conference on 16 April 1940 to decide on the amount of nudity which was to be allowed in theatres. P.S. Le Poer Trench, writing in the *Evening News*, dwelt on the relevant conundrum, 'When is a nude girl not a nude girl?' His solution was when she stood still on a half-lit stage with a wishing well behind her.

In the same month police were trying to stamp out illegal out-of-hours drinking and striptease clubs. They raided the Condor Social Club in Dagenham, housed in a re-conditioned garage, and arrested undercover colleagues posing as dancers.

Billy Hill, king of the London underworld, was released from Chelmsford gaol and celebrated his first night of freedom with established associates – Franny the Spaniel, Horrible Harry, Bear's Breath, Soapy Harry, Tony the Wop and Square Georgie, known collectively as 'The Heavy Mob' – ready to resume lucrative raids on West End jewellers.

TWO

Dunkirk

Getting to the beaches

If you wanted to put a date on the end of 'The Bore War' for Britain it would possibly be 28 May 1940, when the BEF started arriving home from Dunkirk. But, already at this time, the news was bad enough to end any sense that this was not a real war. On 4 April the Germans occupied Denmark in one day and Hitler announced that this country, as well as Norway, was being protected from the 'aggression of the democracies'. Holland surrendered on 15 May and Belgium on 28 May.

Today, historical attention on those who escaped from Dunkirk dominates and it is easy to forget the tens of thousands who were captured trying to get there (no one was left on the beaches alive). Rowland J.S. Young spent five years as a POW and, on capture, had to endure the sarcasm of a 'comic' German officer referring to a song on the current British hit parade:

'So, Tommy, you hang out your washing on the Siegfried Line, yes? England? Caput!'

Valiant holding counter-attacks slowed German progress towards the coast. On 25 May Lance Corporal Edward Doe of the 2nd Battalion of the King's Royal Rifle Corps (KRRC) decided, in some desperation, to let fly with one of the KRRC's most powerful weapons – the 'Boys' anti-tank rifle. He had to be extremely careful: the recoil from the gun could dislocate a shoulder.

The shell hit a Tiger tank and made a plopping noise, rather like a ping-pong ball. Some of the paintwork was damaged.

However, overall, the British counter-attacks were so successful that General von Rundstedt ordered the German 4th Army to halt on 24 May, assuring Hitler that there was absolutely no chance of the Allied armies escaping by sea.

Those who got to the beaches had countless adventures in the wild and chaotic retreat. Harold J. Chalker (5th Battalion, Royal West Kent Regiment) arrived in the village of Benquin soaking wet. He didn't have time to dry his clothes so changed into female attire which he found in a derelict house. Later he dreaded to think what would have happened to him had he been captured – probably shot by the Gestapo as a spy.

Albert Burrows, heading for Dunkirk but desperate for sleep, collapsed into a ditch. Yet his landing was agreeably soft and dry, onto what was apparently a log. In the dawn light he discovered that he was kipping on a dead horse.

As shells crashed down the remnants of the 9th Battalion of the Durham Light Infantry heard exuberant piano-playing coming from a nearby garden. Four enthusiastic soldiers stood in front of the instrument playing their hearts out, bashing out popular tunes, including *We Shall Hang out the Washing on the Siegfried Line*.

Trooper Albert Cheeseman of the 5th Royal Tank Regiment placed a heavily pregnant woman in his lorry and his sergeant delivered the baby. Another member of the tank crew, who had knowledge of horticulture, christened the child *Viola Tricolor* (Latin for wild pansy).

As the rush west became hectic, many troops arrived on the Dunkirk beaches (which also included those at Malo-les-Bains, Bray and La Panne – a stretch of coast about 10 miles long) on various forms of horseback. Bill Flaherty spotted one bloke on a splendid French cavalry beast and a glorious French cavalry helmet. He was loudly applauded on all sides by the retreating rabble and doffed his headgear in reciprocal salute.

'Cheer up, mates!' he bellowed at them. Bill Flaherty reckoned he must have been bomb happy or absolutely pickled by French wine (pinched along with the horse and the helmet).

Considerable numbers of French soldiers were also making rapid tracks for the coast, but a unit of cyclists did find time for some heavy drinking in an *estaminet* in Poperinghe. A few men of the 65th Field Regiment, Royal Artillery, came past with a comrade, Paddy, who had a smashed foot, so they requisitioned one of the bikes stacked outside.

However, the French were not entirely sozzled and came in hot pursuit. When they caught up with the gunners, Signaller Alfred Baldwin gave a shrug of which the cyclists would have been proud and simply pointed to Paddy's foot. The French graciously retreated back to their vino minus a bike.

Elsewhere, Private David Elliot of the 141st Ambulance, Royal Army Medical Corps, was tending wounded French troops, one of whom was terribly constipated.

'Cabernet! Cabernet,' he called out loudly as at last there seemed to be signs of movement, and David rushed up with the bedpan. The poor soul strained and strained and then a seraphic smile crossed his face, indicating success. The medic removed the bedpan and discovered in it a little poo about the size of a rabbit dropping.

On the beaches

If the backs-to-the-wall fighting and haphazard retreat were painful enough the beaches between 28 May and 4 June were absolutely terrifying, as the Luftwaffe and the German artillery attempted to obliterate the BEF and a large contingent of the French army. Any examples of humour in these circumstances were demonstrations of a glorious fortitude in the face of overwhelming defeat.

Douglas Hellings, near the famous Mole (a jetty), which somehow survived the shelling, strafing and bombing to be used for embarkation for five days, remembered a soldier who produced hair clippers in between raids and salvos, and fashioned dozens of haircuts for the beleaguered men – preference given to those who had a few spare fags. If the customer was generous he could even insist on a favourite shape of coiffure and a final flourish.

The Luftwaffe dropped leaflets as well as bombs – 'RAF destroyed', 'All Generals Gone Home', etc., etc., – urging the Allied troops to surrender in their 'hopeless' position. As toilet paper was in short supply the leaflets came in handy.

The weather remained fine for five days, an advantage for the Luftwaffe but even more for the flotilla of small boats coming to the rescue of the Allied armies. John Woollett, an officer of the 23rd Field Company, Royal Engineers, remembered sunny days watching Stuka dive-bombers attacking ships and Hurricanes attacking the Stukas along with the ack-ack. His cockney driver was equally impressed.

'Cor, sir, it's better than a f***ing football match, ain't it?' was his verdict.

Amazingly enough, a handful of civilians appeared in the dunes, usually in the search for food and drink. Claude 'Mush' Noble of the Sherwood Foresters had two tins of mushrooms and a bottle of wine, which he propped up in the sand and then tried to get some sleep. When he awoke the wine was gone and there were sounds of a happy Frenchman singing from behind a bush.

'Shoot the bugger!' a pal suggested to Mush.

'Nah,' he responded. 'He's happy – for now. Leave him out of the war.'

Bombing resumed: Mush's new-found pal from the Devons (the battalions were hopelessly mixed up) surveyed a dogfight in the skies above.

'Ee,' he commented, 'ain't they up a depth!'

Up at La Panne, Alfred Clarke regarded a lonely bandstand. 'Well, I'll go to hell – not even a f***ing band to see us off!'

Embarkation

The desperate men scanned the Channel anxiously for the boat which might be their saviour. The faint outline of a vessel penetrated the early morning mist of 29 May. 2nd Lieutenant Arthur Curtis (7th Field Company, Royal Engineers), who had a long experience of recognising ships due to his father's knowledge and the use of *Jane's Fighting Ships*, identified the craft as a French battleship, probably the Strasbourg. It turned out to be a paddle steamer from Bournemouth. But the engineers weren't fussy.

A major in the King's Own Borderers was drunk and could hardly stand up. Private E. Newbould (from another regiment) joined in the general condemnation of this dereliction of duty at such a critical time.

'You drunken old sod!'

'Stand up, you old git!' shouted another soldier. 'Let's leave the old bastard!'

But the major's servant picked him up bodily and lifted him onto the rowing boat, which was going out to a waiting ship. The petty officer in the rowing boat offered advice to the soldiers: 'I think, lads, that if you turn round the other way to row we'd all be better off.'

Other jolly Jack Tars on the jetty also tried to help. 'Sing, you buggers!' ordered a petty officer. 'If you don't sing you won't bloody-well go home!'

They sang:

Knees up, Mother Brown,
Knees up, knees up,
Don't get the breeze up,
Knees up Mother Brown.

The petty officer tried to get them organised:

'All on my right side, stand up. You, you nut case, sit down. You're on my left side, you cretin!'

Stukas zoomed in from the north.

'Never mind those arse-oles. Now let's try again. All on my right stand up! On my right!'

'Any more for the Skylark!' called a fellow sailor.

Embarkation proceeded.

All aboard

Humphrey Bredin, a company commander of the Royal Ulster Regiment, slid exhausted to the deck of a ferryboat. A steward materialised and asked the commander for his esteemed order. Bredin wanted a beer.

'Sorry, sir, alcohol can only be served beyond the three-mile limit.'

'How can we lose the war with people like that on our side?' mused the commander. He joined the 338,226 troops who escaped from Dunkirk in 222 Royal Navy ships and 800 civilian craft. He got his beer, eventually, and paid for some for all of his men.

Also at sea, Ordinary Seaman Reginald Cannon sprang into action on the minesweeper HMS *Fitzroy*. The order had gone round that anyone without a specific duty at any time should man the machine gun. Reg had always fancied himself as a machine-gunner. He blazed away at two Messerschmitt 109s and blasted the stays away from the main mast. The captain screamed from above.

'Who's the bloody idiot on that bloody gun! Get him off! Get him off, someone, before he sinks the bloody ship!'

In other waters, Thomas 'Darkie' Hammond had just got below deck when a bomb struck the ship. The deck collapsed. Fifty men waited anxiously in the pitch dark as seamen tried to cut through with axes. Darkie also decided to sing:

Cheer up, lads,
F**k 'em all.
You'll get no promotion
This side of the ocean,
So, cheer up lads,
F**k 'em all.

The other forty-nine trapped soldiers joined in joyfully as the sailors broke through and cleared a way to the decks. Two men arrived at the escape hole simultaneously.

'After you, mate.'

'No, after you, mate.'

They were rudely interrupted from behind. 'If you two buggers can't make up your bleedin' minds let some other bugger out!'

They took the hint. The ship was on fire and they all had to jump overboard before they could be rescued by another ship.

On board his ship, Arthur Blakeburn hung up his soaked clothes in the boiler room but someone pinched them, and later he walked along Margate pier wrapped in a towel. Happily, Fred Clapham's clothes remained safe on the hot pipes but he had to hop across a red-hot grid in bare feet to reach them.

Peter Martin, 2nd Lieutenant, and his platoon got on board a whaler heading towards a destroyer, but as they came near it dropped anchor and promptly departed. The padre leapt to his feet and cried out in anguish: 'Lord, lord, why hast thou forsaken us?'

The boat rocked and began to ship water. 'Sit down!' roared the soldiers as one – so loudly that someone on the destroyer heard them and it turned back.

Out at sea the Thames barge *Shannon* passed a ship's boat that was packed with soldiers and being pulled along by a smaller dinghy rowed by members of the Spanish Labour Corps. *Shannon* took on board the Spaniards and left the soldiers to do their own rowing.

Elsewhere, Robert Newborough, running a Fleet Air Arm motorboat, passed a bloke in a canoe. 'What are you doing out here?' called Newborough.

'I've got room for one,' replied the canoeist. This demonstrated how flat the Channel was during those fateful days.

At the same time, a drifter crammed with troops came alongside HMS *Jasper*. 'Can you tell me the way to Dover?' requested the skipper. The navy gave him a course and his boatload gave three loud cheers.

Many men arrived on the beaches having adopted stray dogs. Sadly, and rather callously, the Military Police destroyed them all – except a little French mongrel aboard HMS *Windsor* in the company of Ordinary Seaman Stanley Allen. They successfully landed in Dover and after six months of quarantine the little animal (re-christened Kirk) became a great favourite in Allen's village in Hampshire.

At Ramsgate Station staff called out, 'Any platform, any train', but General Sir Brian Horrocks (very late in leaving the beach despite the claims of German propaganda and rescued out of the sea by a Dutch coastal steamer) was personally directed to a particular train going to Reading, where his family lived. When he awoke he was in Darlington.

Corporal Charles 'Bert' Nash, Royal Army Ordnance Corps, also remembered arrangements in Ramsgate: a regimental sergeant major

'Kirk' escapes from Dunkirk.

(RSM) ordered all soldiers living south of Luton to stand on his left and all those living north of Luton to stand on his right. Those on the left were sent to Chester and those on the right to Aldershot or Chichester.

Back home

They arrived in Dover, Folkestone, Ramsgate, Margate, Newhaven and many other ports. They were ragged, dirty, wet, hungry and thirsty. Countless volunteers rushed forward with food and drink. Even in Headcorn, inland in Kent, survivors collected. Mrs Joan Launder even recalled a black man in baggy white cotton trousers, a red waistcoat and a 'strange' hat.

Cyril L. Beard of the Second Survey Regiment remembered being treated as a hero. For a week or two everything was free – breakfast, dinner, tea, buses, trains, cinemas and much more.

A chum advised him: 'Make the most of it, Cyril, mate. You'll soon be back to normal.'

CHEER UP, MATE!

Dick Cobley, a heavy smoker, didn't have to buy a fag for a month, whizzed around gratis on buses and went to the pictures every day for a fortnight without paying a penny.

The *Daily Mirror* was triumphant: 'BLOODY MARVELLOUS' was its headline.

Winston Churchill made his 'we shall fight in the fields and in the streets' speech, but was overheard muttering at the same time, 'And beat the bastards about the head with bottles, that's all we've got'.

However, survivors were also muttering about the role of the RAF in the great escape. 'Where was the bloody air force?'

Fred Rosier's wife, overhearing this in a train, was able to respond: 'I can tell you where one is right now – in hospital. I'm just going to visit him.'

Pilot Officer Tony Bartley of 92 Squadron told the story of a fellow pilot who was shot down over Dunkirk and swam to a boat.

'Get back!' ordered a seaman. 'We're not picking you up, you bastard! Only the soldiers.'

The fact was that the planes flew high, 20,000ft or more, and were obscured by the great palls of smoke hanging over Dunkirk. Also, many fighters were inland trying to stop the Luftwaffe from reaching the beaches.

Major Donald Wilson-Haffenden eventually reached home in Camberley and fell into a deep sleep only to be awakened by his wife with the tidings that there was an air raid and that they would have to go down to the cellar.

The major said, 'I've been bombed all the way home and I'm not going to any cellar for anyone!'

However, by the time Bombardier Kean reached his next posting after Dunkirk – 56 Heavy Regiment, Royal Artillery in East Sussex – things were getting back to normal. Terry Milligan asked him what Dunkirk was like. 'Like, son?' asked the bombardier. 'It was a f***-up, a highly successful f***-up.'

THREE

The Battle of Britain

We are ready

There was apparently some comfort in the thought that Britain was now alone in the struggle against the Nazis (which rather neglected the existence of the British Empire, not to mention the material help coming across the Atlantic from the United States). Still, the idea of being alone encouraged much bravado – rather like Clint Eastwood's 'Go on, make my day' – 'Go on, Adolf, try it on and see what you get, you bugger!'

Anthony Eden had already announced the formation of the Local Defence Volunteers on 14 May – the LDV, or 'look, dive and vanish', or even the 'Parashots', possibly in reference to the imminent arrival of German paratroopers disguised as nuns.

Even Broadcasting House in London set up its own LDV group, and on 9 June Sir Stephen Tallents strolled over in his pyjamas and dressing gown from his nearby flat to test out the new security measures of the BBC. He reached the boiler room without being challenged and planted a 'bomb', and then returned home for his sherry and *ITMA* and Funf, the spy. It was just as well that in the real world the German spies were being rounded up and invited to spy on the enemy.

On 6 June Squadron Leader 'Spike' O'Brien had to force land near a village in 'Hell's Corner' (north and east Kent) and went into the

LDVs look out for German parachutists on the Sussex Downs, May 1940.

local to phone home. A bloke in a strange uniform (strange to Spike, anyway) was having a drink at the bar.

'Are you Polish – or Czech, perhaps?' enquired Spike politely.

'Oh, no, nothing like that,' said the strange airman, 'I'm a German pilot, actually, old poy. Just been shot down by one of your chaps. Care for a pint, old poy?'

He fished out a great wad of English money.

Home defence

Ipswich was bombed on 18 June and it was Tyneside's turn a few days later. Pilot Officer Nigel Rose crippled a Heinkel which was trying to blow up the Forth Bridge. It landed in a field. Squadron Leader Farquhar followed it down to try and stop the crew setting fire to their bomber. Unfortunately, however, he finished up in a ditch, turned over and was left hanging from the cockpit by his straps.

The Luftwaffe kindly came over to cut him free but all this was suddenly cut short when a deputation of the Women's Land Army came roaring across the turf with a formidable phalanx of pitchforks.

'Don't mess with them,' advised the squadron leader, 'else you'll be in trouble, lads. I would hand over your Lugers, if I were you.'

One glance at the pitchforks convinced the Germans that this was good advice. The Land Army arrested them all, including Farquhar, and marched them smartly into captivity.

The Land Army, which also did valuable work in the Great War, had been re-formed by Lady Denham in April 1939. By the end of that year they were 4,500 strong. Having survived an Arctic winter out in the fields Eileen Grabham (a suitable name) had been expertly trained to milk cows to the tune of 'Good King Wenceslas last looked out in his pink pyjamas', a more suitable pace than that of her original tune, 'Mr. What-you-call-it, what you doing tonight', which had too much pace and produced loud complaints from the cows.

Eileen had also become a competent campaigner against the inveterate enemy of the Land Army, the Auxiliary Territorial Army, or ATS, commonly referring to them as 'officers' groundsheets'. In

Removing the signposts in preparation for invasion, 1940.

spirited response, the ATS advised the Land Army to keep their backs to the ground. It was a good indication that war was doing wonders for women's lib.

In contrast, Acting Pilot Officer Richard Leoline Jones (64 and 19 Squadrons) couldn't persuade a female of any shape or form to dance with him. Finally, in exasperation, he demanded to know from quite a plain ATS girl what was wrong with him.

'You've got V.D.,' she claimed rather brusquely.

'No, I haven't,' he protested indignantly.

'Well, your Sergeant said that anyone with a white armband has got V.D.'

(All acting pilot officers wore white armbands.)

Surviving in June and July 1940

Air-raid warnings came daily. Mr Balditch of Bethenden in Kent developed frayed nerves, or 'queer', as he described them (the word meant 'odd' in those innocent days). On 25 June the siren sounded and Mr Balditch washed his false teeth, climbed into his boots, gathered up his wife's jewels and tore off to the Anderson shelter in the garden. He muttered fiercely to himself as his anxious family watched for further signs of psychological deteriorations.

It was thus with some relief that the all clear sounded. But, no, it was granddad snoring. The anxiety continued as Mr Balditch counted his wife's jewels over and over again and, at one point, made to return to the house when he became convinced that he had left a precious bracelet in the scullery.

'She sold it,' his daughter pointed out.

Mr Balditch shook his head, thoroughly rattled. But he made a full recovery and awaited the Battle of Britain, much of which took place directly over his head.

Operation Sealion, the proposed German invasion of Britain, occupied minds as July wore on. Jim Elkin of the 15th Battalion of the Queen's Royal Regiment was guarding Dover Castle. His commanding officer (CO) told him that the castle had had a sentry for 800 years, Jim reckoned it was about time someone relieved him.

The WAAFs (Women's Auxiliary Air Force) at Detling air base were issued with hockey sticks, but Sylvia Yeatman had a revolver up her stocking which she acquired at the small arms school in Hythe. After all, Winston Churchill had proclaimed on the radio that since the Battle of France was over it was time for the Battle of Britain. At the same time, Sergeant Pilot Bamberger at Biggin Hill made no secret of the fact that he did not really know how to fly his Spitfire properly and his gunnery skills were primitive. He had fired a few shots at the North Sea and managed to hit it.

The air battle was closely reported in cinema newsreels. Referring to the battle over Dover on 19 July the excited commentator almost screamed: 'There's goes another Messerschmitt!' It was, in fact, one of the very cumbersome British Defiant two-seater fighters.

Valiant Polish pilots, such as Karol Priak (nicknamed 'Cognac') and Boleslaw Wlasnowalski (nicknamed 'Vodka') of 32 Squadron, were desperately trying to learn English in order to follow instructions.

The Battle of Britain 'score', according to a newspaper vendor. (Reproduced by kind permission of the Trustees of the Imperial War Museum (HU810))

It helped when Sergeant David Evans, a trainer at 12 Operations Training Unit at RAF Benson, hit on the imaginative idea of teaching the language through the medium of a strip cartoon in the *Daily Mirror* – namely the one featuring Jane, who was usually in a state of undress. The Poles thus made rapid progress, especially in anatomy.

Down on the ground we were still learning the ropes, too. By August I knew that 'Bandits at Angels One-Five' meant Messerschmitt's at 15,000ft, and was lectured by fellow students on the advantages of coming at them out of the sun. 'Pancake' was the word for 'come back and land', 'Vector' gave the correct direction and 'Buster' was 'flat out'.

'Bandits at three o'clock,' I apparently called out in my sleep, dreaming about Stukas.

Technical stuff

Radio and radar became absolutely critical in the Battle of Britain. David Hunt remembered the sophisticated training on Uxbridge's soccer pitch. El Dorado ice-cream tricycles had screens mounted over the handlebars so that David and his pals couldn't see where they were going. They had to pedal furiously to move at all because of the very high gear. They received instructions over RT sets and headphones and steered by compass following the sort of orders I was expert at, such as 'Angels 20', and ones which I didn't know, such as 'pipsqueak'. 'Tally-ho' and 'under bandits' were familiar to me. There were frequent collisions.

Air-raid Precaution Wardens also received training. People from all walks of life volunteered for the vital service. Steve Woodcock had supervised the construction of Waterloo Bridge but he gave his evenings and nights to ARP practices at Ladbroke Grove in West London. For instance, on 24 July he learnt how to assist 'victims' of air raids. Miss Smythe was 'in hysterics' and Miss Orpen had swallowed her false teeth.

Steve and his colleagues carefully laid Miss Orpen on her face and shook her head about, which made her feel sick. She had to retire into the yard. Meanwhile, a retired general with a 'cut hand' was being

Home Guard exercise with 'Nazi' prisoners, 1940.

instructed how to hold the injured limb over a bucket in order to save the carpet.

More news from Glasgow

Back up in Glasgow, Pam Ashford was still valiantly despatching her Mass Observation diary to London. Also on 24 July she was awakened by loud bangs at 6.30 a.m. She considered various possibilities. One: was it thunder? Two: was it the cleansing department? Three: was it ack-ack fire? Four: was it enemy bombs? It turned out to be number four. The city was getting a pasting.

On the next day she reported that a certain Mr Nevis had been summoned to the local police station to answer charges of spreading alarm and despondency through defeatist talk. He had to fork out £20 in bail to get out and find a solicitor. A friend of Pam's admitted that Mr Nevis had distressed her so much that she had to take some brandy.

Tally-ho

Godfrey Winn of the *Sunday Express* visited 54 Squadron on 18 July in order to find out what made the pilots tick. 'Portrayal of a Miracle Man', he called his article. One of these heroes told Winn that the reason he was flying a fighter rather than a bomber was that his trainer discovered that he was pretty good at flying upside down. The same pilot roared with derision at the suggestion that he was 'a knight of the sky'. 'A knight of the night' was nearer the mark. He did reveal that he was hooked on Connie Boswell singing 'Martha'.

On the last day of July Squadron Leader Brian Lane, with eight other Hurricanes, confronted a huge force of German fighters over Hellfire Corner.

'Tally-ho, chaps,' he called cheerily over the intercom, 'target ahead. Come on, chaps, let's surround them!'

That summer, Brian Lane was awarded the Distinguished Flying Cross (DFC) and Douglas Bader pointed to it as they sunbathed on the turf awaiting the warning to take off.

'What's that, old chap?' he asked in mock wonder. 'I must get one of those.'

Elsewhere, Flight Lieutenant Tom Mangan of 43 Squadron bailed out on 8 August but was unable to identify himself to the police in Midhurst. His adjutant came over to provide identification.

'Never seen him before in my life,' he declared loudly, and Tom was sent back to the cells, which were full of German pilots. They were good company as Tom awaited the end of the adjutant's big joke. He had gone for a couple of pints and returned cheerfully a couple of hours later. The station sergeant reluctantly let Mangan go but warned the two airmen about their future conduct. The Germans were rolling about laughing.

The RAF was now desperate for new pilots. Mr C. Tomlin (another M.O. correspondent) had a bath on Thursday 8 August as preparation for his RAF medical on the following Saturday. He was a bit worried because he couldn't touch his toes. Despite this disadvantage he was accepted into the RAF.

William Strachan was from Jamaica and desperate to get across and do his bit for the empire. He sold his bike and his saxophone and thus raised £15 for passage to England on a banana boat belonging to the Jamaican Fruit Shipping Company. The fare left him with just £2 10s in his pocket. The journey took a month but he did have the cabin next to the captain's on this vast and luxurious ship (he found out later that was because it saved on the cleaning bills).

In England he stayed at the YMCA in Tottenham Court Road, the base for many Jamaicans in England. In the morning he walked to Adastral House in Aldwych, quite a sensible thing to do when trying to join the RAF since this was its HQ. He got short shrift from the sentry at the door. 'Piss off,' he said.

But a friendly RAF officer coming in saved the day and he was taken before a sergeant at a desk.

'Where d'you come from?' he asked William.

'Kingston.'

'Well, there's a perfectly good recruiting office in Kingston.'

'No – Kingston, Jamaica.'

The 'Hooray Henry' officer continued to be helpful, however, because he thought Kingston was in West Africa and he liked West Africans. So William was sent for a medical at Euston in a freezing cold room. He passed and the doctor told him to go home and wait for a summons. William pointed out that this was difficult and he had very little money. Within hours he was on the train to the 4 Elementary Flying Training School in Blackpool. The whole recruitment process took a record forty-eight hours. William became a Flight Lieutenant in 99 Squadron.

Free French

The situation would have been worse without the contributions of foreign pilots. René Mouchotte, a pilot, was kept in Oran, North Africa, by Vichy forces. He managed to escape in an 'unserviceable' plane to Gibraltar on 2 July 1940 (a feat announced in *The Times* for 5 March 1941).

On Gibraltar he anxiously awaited confirmation that the RAF would have him. Meanwhile, he entertained himself watching patrols armed with rubber truncheons rounding up dozens of drunken matelots. As they went down another policeman caught them before they hit the pavement.

Mouchotte eventually became a RAF hero (he was a wing commander at Biggin Hill in 1943) but in 1940 he had a lot of training to do. At Salisbury on 29 July – he couldn't pronounce it, 'Soolsbeurre' being his best attempt – he even failed to drive a car on the correct side of the road. To make matters worse he had to push the fighter throttle forward instead of pulling it back.

Sentence of death was passed on Mouchotte and all other Free French pilots unless they returned to Vichy France before 15 August. Their vocabulary progressed at the rate of about one and a half words a week (they were busy men – perhaps they needed Jane). By 5 August, Charles, one of Mouchotte's compatriots, could utter 'Yes', 'No', 'Darling', 'Very nice', 'I love you' and 'That is all – good luck'.

On the evening of 14 August all those sentenced to death attended a grand party in London and all had a great time. During this month from their base at Sutton Bridge the Free French lost on average one pilot a day due to training accidents.

More of August 1940

Flying Officer Geoffrey Page of 52 Squadron was rescued from the Channel (which German pilots called the 'Shit Canal') on 12 August but had lost his trousers and underpants. Waiting on the pier in Margate to greet him was the mayor of the town bedecked in a top hat and tails.

'Welcome to Margate,' he formally greeted the bedraggled hero. From the sheer horror of escaping from a blazing plane, trying to drag open the cockpit shield with burnt hands and then struggling to free himself from his parachute in the sea, here he was greeted by this vision in a top hat.

On the same day, Tilly Rice's two little boys in Epsom were discussing the overall military situation.

Dick said, 'I'd like to kill old Hitler.'

Bob said, 'Oh, you shouldn't do that. That might make the war worser because the people in Germany might wonder where he was.'

In the air, Flight Lieutenant Crook (609 Squadron) overheard a German commander on his intercom on 13 August. 'Achtung! Achtung! Spit and Hurry!'

Wise advice, considered David Crook, because it was the thirteenth day of the month, there were thirteen Spitfires in action and thirteen enemy planes were shot down.

A critical stage in the Battle of Britain was when the Luftwaffe were attacking airfields and radar installations. Radar enabled the RAF to locate the raiders in good time and to get their fighters in the right place at the right time. The extent of damage to airfields has probably been overstated since it was pretty difficult to wipe out a whole airfield. In the event, only Manston, very near the Kent coast, was completely put out of action for any length of time.

But in the summer of 1940 the situation looked very dire. In the early morning of 14 August, 250 bombs were dropped on Eastchurch airfield on the Isle of Sheppey. Flight Sergeant Tofts and Sergeant Cox flung themselves into the nearest shelter: it was a urinal.

'It's not time to be squeamish,' declared Cox, dripping with pee.

On 15 August Flight Lieutenant David Crook of 609 Squadron was again in the air, shooting down a Blenheim bomber, which, as you may know, was one of ours.

The problem was that the Blenheim looked very much like a Junkers 88. True, it was much slower, but the brave pilot imagined he was having a go at a whole swarm of 88s. Just as he was pressing the button Crook did notice that the plane had a gun turret on the fuselage – not a feature of a Ju 88: too late.

Fortunately, the Blenheim pilot managed a crash landing. But subsequently Crook had to endure a lot of leg-pulling. In his defence was the fact that many of his fellow pilots had been worrying about the similarity of the two planes.

As a parting shot on the same day, enemy fighters raked Croydon with machine-gun fire with the result that one suburban lady emerged from her shelter to find her washing shot to pieces.

During August Crook's squadron acquired three American pilots. They had had quite a job persuading the American embassy to let them fly. The diplomats were trying to preserve neutrality, but they were allowed to stay. Their airfield in Dorset was bombed on 24 August and 'Red', one of the Americans, endlessly cheerful and casual, only escaped death or serious injury by flinging himself into a deep chalk pit.

Struggling back after the all clear, covered in chalk and slime, he made one his trademark remarks: 'Aw, hell, I had a million laughs!'

He habitually pointed to his wings and commented, 'I reckon these are a one-way ticket, pal.'

Later, the Americans joined the Eagle Squadron and Red was killed trying to fight off a whole crowd of Messerschmitts.

Invasion scares

Invasion fears were rife by the middle of August but Mrs Tibbs assured Tilly Rice that she felt safe, as, being a Catholic, she had hidden her rosary. She calculated that the invasion would come at 4 p.m. one day next week.

'Meanwhile, in Britain, the entire population has been flung into a state of complete panic'. Cartoon by Pont. (Reproduced with permission of Punch Ltd)

''Ere, Tilly,' she nonetheless worried, 'wot do yer think 'e'll do when 'e gets 'ere?'

'Why, Mrs. Tibbs,' Tilly assured her, 'he'll come straight out to Epsom to rape you.'

'Wot – me?' Mrs Tibbs shook her head emphatically. 'Oh, no, no man's been near me for fifteen years and 'e's not going to start.'

An equally defiant lady filled her car with pepper pots to blind any German who came after her. There was still a strong rumour going round that the Germans would arrive as nuns. Real nuns had quite a distressing time going about their business. Moreover, anyone carrying a haversack was suspected of harbouring a parachute.

The prime minister continued to urge everyone to be brave, paying tribute to the RAF: 'Never in the field of human conflict was so much owed by so many to so few,' he boomed.

One of 'the few' listening in thought Churchill was referring to his squadron's mess bills.

More details of Operation Sealion are now known. Joachim von Ribbentrop, the Nazi Foreign Minister, was promised Cornwall by Hitler. Von Ribbentrop loved this part of the world, especially St Ives and St Michael's Mount. It was also planned to move Nelson's Column to the Fatherland.

There were also detailed plans for the defence of the capital. Pillboxes were disguised as tea stalls, for example. The Home Guard were very

A pillbox disguised as a café near Chelsea Bridge, 1940.

active in this field. The 57th Surrey Home Guard in Mitcham were responsible for an outer defence line and enormous anti-tank trenches were dug across Hackbridge Junction.

In addition, the Mitcham militia had all sorts of surprises for Tiger tanks, such as creeping up at night and despatching sentries and sticking bombs on the tracks. If the German crew emerged in the morning to repair the damage, the further plan was to throw sulphuric acid balls at them. Trip wires were also envisaged, designed to behead motorcyclists.

Still, rumours persisted. One which still had legs was that 30,000 German invaders had been drowned in the 'Shit Canal'. A.P. Herbert in *Punch* had to deny that submarines had appeared in Tunbridge Wells.

How we won

Hordes of enemy fighters were being destroyed between 13 August and 18 August, and so on the 19th the survivors decided to stay at home. Pilot Officer Willy Walter was himself shot down over the sea on 26 August. At the RAF hospital in Halton the surgeon prised an armour-piercing bullet out of Willy's leg and it whizzed past the surgeon's head and pranged the ornamental ceiling.

Legions of sturdy English ladies and the 'few' came into direct contact on the last day of August when Tom Vigars was unable to bale out of his damaged plane – the instrument panel and the control column were shattered – because he was over the centre of London. Eventually he managed to flop down in a field and cartwheeled along until coming to rest in the hedge of a garden. A lady appeared, mug in hand.

'Are you alright, dear,' she asked sweetly. 'Look, have a cup of tea. It'll steady your nerves.'

Down on the ground, RAF personnel continued to try and enjoy themselves between operations. Pilot Officer John Kendal, known as 'Durex' for some obscure reason, could mimic any known celebrity voice, including those of his commanders. It took a lot to silence him. Whilst Sergeant Duggie Hunt looked forward to a post-war revolution following which the country would be governed by pilots (we could have done worse). Continued influence from Hollywood was strong: girls were now being called 'dames' or 'broads'.

Meanwhile, local pubs became shrines: the CO at Biggin Hill mounted up a tannoy system on his car and gave his orders whilst still a mile or so away from the White Hart at Brasted.

'This is the C.O. I want three scotches and two pints of bitter.'

At closing time all serious drinkers retired to Red House, the home of Sir Hector Macneath, to be hosted by his two beautiful daughters.

At the same time, Charles Fenwick at Tangmere went on his own version of a pub-crawl accompanied by a 35-year-old married woman (whose husband was away in the north somewhere). In one bar, scrabbling in her handbag for her fags, she pulled out a Dutch cap and placed it on the bar.

So we won the Battle of Britain. Air Minister Sir Archibald Sinclair came to Kenley, to 64 Squadron, to add his congratulations to those of the prime minister:

'I doff my hat to the Hurricane pilots of 12 Group,' he said to the assembled airmen.

Pilot Officer Richard Jones, along with all the others, was a bit bewildered. Here they were standing in front of their Spitfires ... the bloody old fool couldn't tell a Spitfire from a Hurricane. Also, his knowledge of Fighter Command Groups was equally defective.

He was not alone in making this sort of error, however. After the war, Peter Townsend of 85 Squadron met a German pilot he had shot down.

'Very pleased to meet the Spitfire pilot who shot me down,' he greeted Townsend. 'I flew Hurricanes,' Townsend pointed out.

'Please,' pleaded the Luftwaffe pilot, 'please tell any Germans you meet that you flew a Spitfire', which was very unfair to Hurricanes.

Surviving Battle of Britain pilots were instantly hailed as heroes and Biggin Hill became something of a media centre where (handsome) pilots gave endless interviews. BBC documentaries were written in posh talk (omitting all obscenities) and Hollywood style.

'I'll teach you some manners, Hun.'

'I say, chaps, that was a wizard prang.'

The Air Ministry got a cut of the fees.

There were particular heroes: Paddy Finucane got bags of fan mail, including a note from a Land Girl 'Amongst the turnips, Wiltshire'. At the time, Paddy was in hospital, having eluded the Luftwaffe but not a wall during the blackout.

In real life, Tom Vigars recalled, 'I was shit scared from the word go.'

Tom also suffered from 'bedspin' or the 'phantom pilots', especially after getting blind drunk and crashing into bed. On one of these occasions he answered a call for an extra volunteer pilot and went aloft in red pyjamas and shot down a Heinkel.

'I wasn't fighting for the King,' reckoned Pilot Officer Bob Doe of 234 and 238 Squadrons. 'I was fighting for me Mum – I didn't want them over here.'

The Home Guard played its part

The Local Defence Volunteers had been on red alert with broom handles. It was soon renamed as the Home Guard. Alan Finnimore

'Nell' takes her LDV proficiency test, 25 July 1940.

was actually armed to the teeth with a bow and arrow, and others in his unit had scythes and 'hun-busters' – maces studded with 6in nails. One section leader was elected due to the fact that he was the best rabbit-shooter for miles around.

Another factor in favour of the Home Guard was an average age in excess of 60. Private John Shelton made the telling point that they were too old to run away from the Hun, although there were a number of roller-skating units in London and trained dogs that could run. They were ready to ram Tiger tanks with sections of disused tramlines.

Private Donald Smith was personally not too sure what damage they could inflict on the enemy, but he knew they put the fear of Christ up him. The Home Guard suffered 768 deaths and 5,750 injured without the appearance of the Wehrmacht.

Proper uniforms took time to arrive. A survey of early headgear included homburgs, trilbies, porkpies, cloth caps, bowlers, moleskin caps with earflaps, straw boaters, berets and early Victorian deerstalkers.

Leslie Kershaw remembered the Swanley Railway Home Guard in Kent with great affection. As a 15-year-old he spent many happy hours in the old station booking office. On occasions, the sergeant got fed up with the lack of action and ordered them out on a route march – 200yds up to the top of the hill and 200yds back again.

'Stand at ease!' he ordered upon their return before someone broke wind violently and they all tried it out like claps of thunder.

Yet they were soon to be run off their feet: the Blitz had arrived.

FOUR

The Blitz

7 September 1940

The 1940/41 football season was under way at the Den (Millwall's ground in south-east London) on Saturday 7 September. It was a gloriously sunny day with temperatures over 90°F recorded. Towards the end of the match spectators were set a problem: should they concentrate on the game or follow the myriad dogfights taking place in the skies above the River Thames?

At the nearby greyhound track there was the same dilemma: the dogs on the ground or those above? They had seen air battles before but not on this scale.

A couple of miles further north I was still out playing at around four in the afternoon when the air-raid warning sounded. I hurried towards home and was on the raised pavement in Harbinger Road in the real Millwall on the Isle of Dogs when I heard and saw a swarm of bombers making straight for me (the u-bend in the river which houses the Isle of Dogs was called the 'U-Bogen' by the Luftwaffe). The picture seen here was taken early in the morning of 7 September, when I was asleep with my family in the Anderson shelter: X marks the spot.

My mystery of a year earlier was solved. They would not come along the number 57 or number 56 bus routes, they came straight over the river. Our house was about 400yds south of Millwall Docks

Heinkel 111 bomber over the Isle of Dogs at 6.48 a.m. on 7 September 1940. X marks the spot where the author is sleeping. (Reproduced by kind permission of the Trustees of the Imperial War Museum (C5422))

and the target that day was the docks. But the big bend only suffered lightly in comparison to Bermondsey, Woolwich, Deptford, Poplar and Wapping. Goering sent 300 bombers and 600 fighters to do the job.

Bombs had fallen on London before 7 September. On 24 August a raid on Shorts aircraft factory in Rochester was planned, but (possibly due to a navigational error) the bombs fell on Oxford Street, the City, Stepney, Finsbury, Bethnal Green and East Ham.

On 26 August Wellington bombers had attacked Berlin, but generally missed. They did better on 28, 30 and 31 August and Hitler was not amused – he was still hoping to do a deal with Britain.

A few days before the 7th, on 4 September, Joan Veazey married the curate of St Mary's Church, near the Imperial War Museum. The siren had sounded but everybody was determined to carry on with the wedding. The ceremony was completed and they all stood for photos outside, when a bomb fell in the churchyard.

'Never mind,' shouted the intrepid photographer, 'just smile, then we can clear off.' The bridegroom's mother whistled the wedding march.

Miss Stansfield, not many miles away, was pushed to the ground by a complete stranger to save her from the blast of a nearby explosion. She remembered being worried about her only pair of stockings. She eventually married this saviour. The Blitz, indeed, was a useful dating agency: Lucy Brown-Smith met her future spouse in a brick shelter.

Back to the 7 September where I was now safely ensconced in my Anderson shelter but wondering: where on earth was Flight Lieutenant 'Rockfist' Rogan (of the *Champion* comic) with his gloved fist on the joystick when he was needed? Where was Captain James Biggleswade ('Biggles') – the character created by Captain W.E. Johns in 1932?

Jim Wolveridge was sheltering in the crypt of a church in Stepney. He remembered the second wave of bombers coming over at ten minutes past eight. There was no light in the crypt but through the high windows they could see the huge fires sweeping over Dockland: wharves, warehouses and shipping was going up in flames. Next to Jim an accordionist played *Roll out the barrel, we'll have a barrel of fun*, a song that became the anthem of the Blitz.

ARP Wardens were having a barrel of fun pulling people out of blazing houses in Cubitt Town. They addressed some of them as 'mate': these were the ones they knew and liked.

'Cheer up, mate,' they tried to console the dazed and dust-covered victims. 'Have a cup of tea, mate.'

Others, less popular, were called 'mister' or 'missus', but still offered some tea. However, if you were 'sir' or 'lady' you had to get your own brew.

A local vicar was interviewed in his church. 'Was anyone in the church, Rev?' asked a warden.

'No – why?' responded the vicar. 'Has it gone?'

'Yes, Rev, mate.'

'Oh dear,' sighed 'Rev mate', 'unemployed.'

A member of the aristocracy was being driven across London by his chauffeur to a West End appointment. 'Shall I put my tin hat on, John?' he asked the driver.

'I think so, sir,' advised John.

Tom Bellis, a 12-year-old boy living in Hackney was exceedingly less fortunate than I was. The public shelter he was in suffered a direct hit and a piece of shrapnel passed through his skull. As he tried to crawl through the rubble a woman under a blanket accosted him.

'Don't get blood on my blanket!' she scolded him. Tom was searching for his mother. In hospital, a few days later, he was told by his father, home on compassionate leave from the forces, that his mother was dead. It was Tom who had persuaded her to go to the shelter.

The day after

The morning of 8 September dawned: did you have a house left? Did you get bomb blast and have a massive clearing-up job to do? Doreen, in Cubitt Town, cheerfully swept up the mess.

'Well,' she philosophised, 'there's one thing about all this – it keeps you busy and you forget about the war.'

Another housewife was equally calm. 'Do you know what, my dear,' she told her old man, 'I've never known the content, at times, the real happiness I've known since the war started.'

On this day, Operation Cromwell was set in motion – preparation for a German invasion. Indeed, the church bells at Stoke Abbot indicated that it had actually started. The local volunteers at the Women's Voluntary Service (WVS) hut wondered what they should do first.

'What about putting the kettle on?' suggested Julia Whitfield.

'Are you thinking of giving the Germans a cuppa?' wondered her friend.

In East Anglia the Home Guard were also sure the Germans had arrived and they blew up strategic bridges. Young Donald Wheal, now back in Chelsea, agreed with Churchill that they should fight on the

Holland House Library, London, after an air raid in 1940.

beaches – or at least Lots Power Station down by the river, a favourite haunt of his.

The newspapers were still delivered on 8 September. The *Daily Express* had an advert on its back page:

No Act of Parliament compels you to look after yourself. It's up to you. The first and foremost step is to keep your bowels open and your kidneys well flushed. Kruschen does this for you in the simplest possible way.

Perhaps with bombs falling keeping your bowels open was the least of your problems. It was not quite so dodgy in Kensington where Joan Wyndham was in a shelter with the literary figure, Sir John Squires, who was roaring drunk and having words with his Presbyterian cook.

Joan's M.O. diary entry for 8 September indicated that she lost her virginity on that day. But she was not impressed.

'Don't you like my cock?' demanded her boyfriend peevishly, but she recorded her serious lack of enthusiasm for the new-found act. She would have preferred a decent fag or a good film.

'Rockfist' and 'Biggles' were not the only missing elements of defence on the Isle of Dogs. Bill Rogers at the Heavy Rescue Depot bemoaned the lack of anti-aircraft fire on the island. There was one gun and they had to put it on the back of a lorry and tear round the island firing from different places – mainly in order to convince the locals that something was being done.

East Enders took shelter on the Underground and the authorities could do nothing about it. Bedding and valuables were hidden in suitcases. It was every man, woman and child for themselves. Children were sent off early in the day to book places for the night. They were all down there before the trains stopped for the night and police and staff had to go round moving arms and legs out of the way.

Some bombs did drop in Hyde Park. In this part of the world people had servants.

'They've hit Westminster Bridge, ma'am,' announced one housemaid.

'Oh, how awful,' said the lady of the house. 'Is it in the river?'

'It's a pub, mother,' sighed Josephine Russell, her daughter.

Goering sent only 200 bombers that day – targeting power stations and railway lines. Elizabeth Harris in North London didn't need any air-raid warnings. Her cat was a feline early warning system. It must have been the vibrations: she suddenly tore up the garden and into the Anderson into a prime place at the back.

And so it goes on – September and October

There were no raids on 9 and 10 September, then one every day until 4 October and then every night until 2 November. Other cities also suffered and life became difficult for milkmen. George Beardmore was at his wit's end.

'My 'orse's all knackered running rahnd and rahnd dodging the bleedin' bombs,' he complained peevishly to George. ''E's gone right orf 'is grub 'e 'as.'

Stephen Spender came to our school to describe his work with the Auxiliary Fire Service but we were more interested in the fact that his name sounded like 'suspender'. Donald Wheal and his mates fought back with song:

> Hitler, he's only got one ball,
> Goering, he's got none at all,
> Himmler, he's very similar.

On 13 September a lone bomber raided Buckingham Palace but the bomb failed to detonate and it was carried along the stately corridors on a stretcher. The queen now believed that she could 'look the East End in the face'.

On 20 September the famous tenor Richard Tauber was singing at the Alhambra. On stage he approached the lead soprano full of passion and swept into his aria. 'The siren has just sounded,' he sang.

The Home Guard still performed gallantly when Sergeant Pilot P.H. Fox of 56 Squadron crashed on 30 September (during the last mass German bomber raid) and a detachment of the Home Guard came hurtling across a field.

'British! British! British!' he almost screamed because a fellow pilot had been shot in the foot by the Home Guard on the previous day. Another pilot was set upon by highly trained Home Guard Alsatians and bullmastiffs.

Fire-watchers were just as diligent. Catherine Phipps-Nune was struggling home in the blackout when she was accosted by one hanging in a tree. Whether he thought Catherine was a fire hazard or a spy was not clear, but he wasn't taking any chances.

'Halt! Who goes there?' he called.

'It's me, Catherine Phipps-Nune.'

'You've got to say 'friend' or 'foe'.'

'Friend or foe.'

'No – which one?'

'Friend.'

'Advance six paces, friend, and put up your hands.'

'I can't, I'm holding me handbag.'

Another woman groping through the blackout was Joan Buchanan, a society deb and ambulance driver. Indeed, most of the ambulances were driven by middle-class ladies since they had already learnt to drive. Joan could be shopping in the West End during the day and later dining at the Ritz (even being presented to the king) prior to doing a twelve-hour stint in her ambulance attired in a plain cotton coat and hat. She helped to carry corpses and the injured on stretchers. Driving in blacked-out streets with only small sidelights was a nightmare.

Disruption of civilian life

George Beardmore, an M.O. diarist, was a senior billeting officer in Harrow and his main job was to sort out accommodation for bombed-out people. A local gravedigger suffered this fate. Beardmore was somewhat surprised to discover that the gravedigger's wife lived upstairs and another woman downstairs. The story was that the wife had been committed to a mental asylum before the war and the gravedigger had acquired a new family – lady friend and children. But the asylum ran out of funds and was forced to return the gravedigger's wife to him. Regulations from the Home Office were clear: in no circumstances must citizen's morals be questioned in any local council investigations. Accordingly, Beardmore re-housed the gravedigger, his wife, girlfriend and children in exactly the same way as they had been found.

Harold Brush, another M.O. diarist, was trying to buy a book in Charing Cross Road on 5 October but every time he went into a shop the siren sounded and the assistants ushered everyone out and put up the shutters. Between Leicester Square and Tottenham Court Road there were seven raids – all imaginary. Later, he went into his local public shelter where his bunk was so narrow he fell out every time he turned over in his sleep.

Indeed, night raids meant many sleepless nights. On 15 October the raids lasted from 8 p.m. to 5 a.m., and there were 900 fires to put out in London. But as the nights passed the number of planes coming over got smaller and smaller.

'What's the matter, Adolf?' sneered one Mrs Wright. 'Running out of planes, are you?'

She lived in Bouverie Street in East Ham. That night, Adolf had his own back and burst the gas main in her street. She shrugged and took her kettle out and boiled it on the hot pipe. Yes, they were getting used to the Blitz and 'bomb bores' were given short shrift.

''Ere, dear,' a housewife informed her neighbour in Poplar, 'I was 'avin a cup of tea when this incendiary rolled in the back door and so I did no more that 'it it with me rolling pin. But it bounced up and went in me sink ...'

'Put a sock in it, mate,' interrupted her neighbour rudely. 'You've already bleedin' told me that and everybody in the road. If you 'it a bleedin' incendiary with a bleedin' rolling pin you wouldn't be out 'ere telling the story.'

You could wear a badge with 'I've got a bomb story, too' printed on it. Joan Veazey did have a good story, in addition to her adventures at her wedding. On the night of 27 October a bomb fell on a chemist's shop and blew a load of sanitary towels up in the trees. Early morning workers made a number of (rude) comments about the hanging pads, but the curate's wife was of the bulldog breed and she clambered up aloft and removed the offending articles.

During the same raid Mrs Cecilie Eustace was in an ARP shelter in Chiswick. She wasn't taking cover: she was in there two nights a week as a volunteer but after she had finished her duties and on her nights off she slept on a pew in the local church. The idea was to escape the terrible pong in the shelter.

I have first-hand experience of similar aromas. People ran along our street holding their chamber pots (po's), but quite frequently in situ toilet systems broke down, especially if you were in there from 8 p.m. to 5 a.m. Cecilie clearly preferred bombing to being asphyxiated.

If you did stay indoors it could be tricky. A house in Kentish Town was struck on 2 November whilst the lady of the house was having a bath in the prescribed 5in of water. The front wall collapsed, the floor dipped alarmingly and bath and occupant slid effortlessly into the street without shedding a drop of the precious water.

In Belfast, Miss Marsh stayed in her home: under the kitchen table on a mattress in her fur coat clutching her valuables to her bosom.

The royal family continued to brave it along with their subjects, and Norman Hartnell, the royal dressmaker, created a special gown for the queen to wear during night raids. It was kept in a black velvet case with her gas mask. For visiting bomb-damaged areas she did not choose to wear black but preferred a dusty pink, or dusty blue or dusty lilac number.

Famous shelters

Perhaps the most well-known shelter was the Tilbury in Stepney, despite the fact that not all of it was underground. As many as 16,000 shelterers were in there on some nights (Chislehurst Caves could accommodate 15,000). The Tilbury had a certain reputation: it was the first port of call for policeman looking for ne'er-do-wells and prostitutes. There was cold fried fish for sale, fights, courting couples and servicemen on leave (or deserters).

Part of the Tilbury was Liverpool Street Station goods yard. When the gates were opened every night, a mob-like crowd surged down the slope in the race for the best places. Sanitary 'arrangements' were appalling.

Well-heeled tourists, after an evening out in the West End and perhaps dinner at the Savoy, came east to stare at and savour it all – a sort of vicarious thrill. They could return to the Dorchester Hotel where flashlights and slippers were provided in case of a raid.

Alternatively, at the Hungarian Restaurant in Lower Regent Street you could book a shelter as well as a table. In addition, if you were there all night, breakfast was served. But in Christ Church, Spitalfields, it was a case of lifting up the lids of the sarcophagi, scraping out any remaining bones or dirt, and making yourself comfortable. It was certainly warmer in there on cold nights.

Life in the Underground did improve. At Bermondsey Station there was a weekly discussion group, on topics such as 'should women have equal pay for equal work?' Official earplugs were issued to cut

Lifebuoy saves the day after a night in the air-raid shelter. (Reproduced by kind permission of the Trustees of the Imperial War Museum (HU36149))

out the noise of the trains. ENSA (Entertainments National Service Association – or Every Night Something Awful) performed. At West Ham Lever Brothers had a van offering free Lifebuoy soap and showers to people as they emerged bleary-eyed and dishevelled from the shelters.

In the air (some of the time)

Fighter Command continued to shoot down hordes of German bombers and fighters. Their own losses were still heavy. On 7 October Flight Lieutenant David Crook (609 Squadron) landed in a field in Dorset and a large crowd of soldiers and police surged forward in a race to play host. The police triumphed and carried Crook off to the local and plied him with beer (and other drinks) until closing time. They carried him back, unconscious, to his airfield.

Following that, Crook had time off in London. At Lyons Corner House in Coventry Street he scoffed eggs and bacon and befriended a jolly Canadian. Suddenly, there was a tremendous crash and all the windows caved in and the building shook. But those enjoying their meal barely looked up for a second and quickly resumed their conversations.

Also on 7 October a Polish pilot in Crook's squadron shot down a Messerschmitt 109. He watched the pilot bale out, hit the deck and lay there inert.

'I circle round,' Novi told David Crook. 'Bloody German lies there, he is dead. But I look again, he is sitting up, no bloody good.' For Poles the only good German was a dead one.

As another diversion, Crook flew to Wales to pick up a tiny drone which his CO had purchased. It had a 10hp Ford engine and could just about keep up with the birds. Over Salisbury Plain he joined a convoy of lorries and shook hands as he flew alongside them.

Early one morning in October four German pilots walked into a village near Shaftesbury in Dorset and surrendered. No plane could be found although a Dornier had landed on mudflats near Ipswich (130 miles away). The plane was empty and no crew could be found.

What had happened, apparently, was that the Dornier had taken part in a raid on Liverpool but electric storms upset their compass without them realising it. They actually reached France, which they thought was England, and flew back to England, which they thought was France, ran out of petrol and baled out. The plane continued by automatic pilot ('George') to Ipswich.

René Mouchotte was now in 615 Squadron at Northolt – the 'Churchill Squadron'. On 9 December he had to make an emergency landing, hitting a lorry, but 'not violently'. He had to travel back to Northolt by train with his parachute on his back, in a flying suit and boots. He got a lot of funny looks: he could have been the Luftwaffe, especially as he was still struggling with his English.

New fighter pilots were qualifying all the time but after the night raids started, unless they were night fighters, they were going to be disappointed. Sergeant R.A. Wilkinson was a member of

616/619 Squadron. He managed to sum-up the feelings of the 'unlucky few':

'I shot nothing down and no one shot me down,' he said. 'It was a no-score draw.'

November 1940

On 4 November Glasgow was again under attack and Pam Ashford observed looters swarming over bombed houses following rumours that £2,000 had been sown into a pair of pink corsets.

Dogs were under pressure in the city: Pam's friend, Margaret, grew increasingly alarmed as her pet's psychological condition worsened. In order to cheer him up she spread her entire ration of butter over his biscuits, provided him with daily doses of chopped up pig's liver, her entire ration of eggs plus a bar of Cadbury's chocolate. But Rover showed little signs of improvement while Margaret entered a state of semi-starvation.

Down in Hackney, London, Betty Winehouse's dad hung his only pair of trousers on the bedpost overnight, his usual practice, but a blast from a bomb blew them straight out of the window, hotly pursued by Charlie Winehouse before some cheap sod stole them. Betty cracked up.

Nerves were also frayed in the basement shelter at 2a Stanley Crescent, Ladbroke Grove, West London. Stephen Woodcock, ARP Warden (and famous architect), was getting quite fed up with an old blighter attired in a dressing gown and a skullcap, and known to all as 'Poona-Poom'. On the night of 12 November Poona-Poom demanded that Mr Woodcock should immediately telephone Fighter Command to inform them that there were unidentified flares over Shepherd's Bush. As he went on, and on, there were dark mutterings from other established residents of the shelter. Then the old devil said it was his idea of a joke before Stephen Woodcock told him it wasn't funny and no one was laughing. Poona-Poom called them a load of miserable old sods and Stephen had a job trying to persuade Jim Thompson not to hit the eccentric character.

Gradually, public shelter life became more organised – tickets to control entry, cleaning rotas, latrine orderlies etc. At 'Mickey's Shelter' in Stepney (with room for more than 10,000) self-help and democratic leadership was the reward for the sterling work of Mickey Davies, a hunchback dwarf. The shelter was transformed from a huge, stinking warehouse into a well-run, habitable and welcoming safe space.

The improvement here must have some influence on the desire for better conditions at the Tilbury shelter nearby. A deputation of concerned local citizens went to the local ARP HQ to protest about the state of the shelter. Sadly, they were charged by mounted police waving batons about. But things did get better at the Tilbury – slowly.

From Swiss Cottage Underground Station articulate requests for better amenities were passed back and forth between the Ministry for Health, the local council and London Transport. But soon there were 'refreshment specials' on the Underground system taking tea, cocoa, sausage rolls, pies, cakes and buns from station to station. Even George Formby came down below and played his ukulele as part of nightly ENSA concerts.

In Chislehurst Caves electric lighting was installed, proper toilets were built and the cave floors were levelled off. Before that was done, it was a bit like rock-climbing down there.

Other heroes were those brave few who traversed cities de-fusing unexploded bombs (UXB). Lieutenant Horace Taylor, RNVR, was a specialist in sorting out magnetic mines, which weighed 2,000 kilos, were 2ft or more in diameter and 9ft long. His armoury of technological gear consisted of hairpins, matchsticks, bent nails, a bicycle pump and the rubber bulb of a motor horn.

One day in the Blitz there was an unexploded magnetic mine found in the grounds of a large hospital in North London. Horace de-activated it with these sophisticated tools and then blew his whistle to indicate the all-clear. A whole mob of nurses rushed from the hospital bent on grabbing souvenirs from the event: the mine parachute quickly disappeared (to re-appear later as several pairs of silk knickers).

But the girls wanted more, Horace was a bit of a hunk and they wanted some of him. His tie went, then his shirt, shoes, and he had to fight like mad to keep his trousers.

The next mine he attended blew up and tossed him through two houses and did rip off all his clothes. He thought his sight had gone, too. But in the hospital (not the same one as before – just as well because heaven knows what the nurses would have taken this time) they cleared the muck out of his eyes and his sight returned. All Lieutenant Taylor wanted to do was to get back to his boss in order to explain what he thought had gone wrong. He was a consummate professional.

'You can't leave in this condition,' insisted the doctor. 'There might be reactions. Anyway, you haven't got any clothes.'

'You are obstructing a naval officer in the course of his duty,' claimed the brave man, so they found him a medical orderly's shirt and a pair of cook's trousers and off he tore. He didn't like getting beaten by any old magnetic mine.

Operation Trickle

By now a second exodus of children from the cities was under way. But 'exodus' is not a fair description; it was Operation Trickle. After the frustrating experiences during The Bore War parents were far less keen to go or let their children go into the country. But young Bill Reed did go from West Ham and learnt how to skin a rabbit and play golf under the tutelage of the world champion, Henry Cotton, on the course in Little Gidderson, near Hemel Hempstead.

An Exeter Corporation bus conveyed some kids from Reading from the station to the evacuee distribution centre. The driver was rather uncharitable. 'This bleedin' lot are all bedwetters,' he announced to the potential hosts. There had been one or two accidents during the journey.

There were now no more bananas in Britain – or, at least, very few, and these were prohibitively expensive. But we still had Winston Churchill. Edward Morrow, the CBS War Correspondent in London, described the great man to his readers across the Atlantic: in his vast siren suit he looked like a large grey barrage balloon with a cigar.

Lord Haw-Haw had a different line on the Allied leader, alleging that he had only got into power through a conspiracy organised by Lord

Children playing as air-raid wardens, 1941. (Reproduced by kind permission of Mirror Syndication Ltd)

Rothschild and Lord Portal to make vast profits out of compulsory insurance against air raids.

The name 'Lord Haw-Haw' was coined by the Weston Brothers, a comic song duo on the music halls and wireless. One of their patter melodies of 1940 went 'Lord Haw-Haw, the Humbug of Hamburg, the comic of Eau-de-Cologne'.

The 'Humbug of Hamburg', as well as conspiracy theories, had a nice line in details. He warned the pontoon school in the canteen at the Bristol Aeroplane Company in Filton that they would be forced to find a new venue following the imminent raid from the Luftwaffe. This may have indicated a meticulous espionage triumph except for the fact that all works canteens had pontoon schools.

Great Fire of London #2

On the night of 29 December 1940 hundreds of incendiary canisters were dropped on the City of London. Great swathes of the vast commercial centre were reduced to rubble as the fire-fighters waited for the Thames tide to come in. On the South Bank a quarter-mile strip of warehouses and residencies were burnt and destroyed.

St Paul's Cathedral was saved through the dedicated and heroic work of its team of fire-wardens. Apparently, the main qualifications for this volunteer job was a head for heights and a taste for acrobatics.

There was an extensive public grapevine on how to deal with incendiary bombs, a severe peril for cities mainly constructed in the nineteenth century. Indeed, there were numerous theories expounded in Mass Observation diaries. It was generally considered best to throw them out of the window, if you could. Unfortunately, this advice often came without the additional caution to do this with a long-handled shovel.

Meanwhile, we continued to win the espionage war. When the Gloucester Place flat of Tyler Kent was raided in West London (he was a cipher clerk at the US Embassy) they found copies of 1,500 British and American diplomatic telegrams, including many exchanges between President Roosevelt and Winston Churchill. Allied and German cryptographers alike, however, were unable to de-cipher Churchill's signing-off message, 'KBO'. It meant, in fact, 'Keep Buggering On'. Down in his command bunker below Whitehall his telephone operator took his calls. The operator was one Norman Wisdom of the Royal Corps of Signals. As the New Year dawned Norman was put on a charge for referring to the prime minister, rather publicly, as 'Winnie'.

FIVE

North Africa 1940-41

Musso on the move

In June 1940 Italy declared war on Britain and occupied Kassala in the Anglo-Egyptian Sudan. On 13 September they crossed into Egypt from Libya, threatening the coastal town of Sollum.

Alan Moorehead, the famous war correspondent of the *Daily Express*, accompanied a squadron of Blenheim bombers attacking Kassala. Air crew had taken the precaution of issuing him with an information card to use in the event of a crash landing. It was printed in Amharic and English explaining that the holder was a British officer and requested that he should be fed and watered.

But his pilot was dismissive: 'The bastards can't even read their own f***ing language,' he said to Moorehead. 'They'll probably slice you up first and ask questions afterwards.'

In August, Moorehead and other correspondents, including Richard Dimbleby, were at Khashm el Girba in East Africa listening to the BBC World Service from a wireless propped up in a thorn bush providing them with out-of-date news about British military preparations in East Africa.

Moorehead was back on the North African coast later that month as the Italians got ready to capture Sollum. The British commander decided to retire from the town as the Italian artillery started to bombard it. The British engineers had planted mines in every street with detonating wires to their new position outside the town. Every time an Italian shell landed in the town (all the civilians had fled for their lives) the engineers simultaneously detonated a mine some distance away from where the shell had landed.

This caused an angry exchange of words between the Italian Air Force, who were telling the gunners where to fire their shells, ground observers and artillery officers. None of them were able to explain why each shell produced two explosions. Ground observers cast doubt on the Air Force's eyesight and the artillery thought the observers were going mad. It did not auger well for Italian designs on Egypt.

However, they did eventually move very cautiously into the town, where more arguments ensued between the artillery and the observers. Whilst they were debating their next move a message came through from Mussolini to say that he was going to attack Greece and needed men and guns from Libya to do it.

Fight back

They nevertheless advanced with depleted forces to Sidi Barrani, 60 miles inside Egypt, but a battle on 9 December caused them to retreat. There were heavy casualties on both sides, including the most popular prostitute inside Sidi Barrani. She was buried in the military cemetery with full military honours for services rendered to troops regardless of whose side they were on.

Outside the town the advancing British discovered a large bust of Mussolini on the crest of a prominent hill, set on an imposing plinth. It had a gold inscription – a quote from one of his heroic speeches in Genoa: 'He who does not keep moving is lost.' So the unimpressed British soldiers knocked the bust off its plinth and played bowls with it.

They were back in Libya by 17 December and captured Bardia in the New Year 1941, taking 35,949 prisoners. However, the rather elusive and legendary General Bergonzoli escaped with the remnants of his army to Tobruk.

The Royal Engineers put up a splendid new bridge at Mersa Matruh and the war correspondents came bowling along in their truck, Richard Dimbleby driving, and struck it, denting a number of girders.

The Engineers' captain was not happy about it. 'I've been here for a month in this dump building that bridge. I've even just put up a plaque saying "Bridge begun by the 21st Company of the Royal Engineers December 1940. Completed January 1941".'

'Why don't you add "Demolished by War Correspondents January1941"?' suggested Dimbleby.

'Never mind,' sighed the sporting Engineer, 'have a cup of tea.'

On 22 January British and Australian forces captured Tobruk and another 25,000 Italians. The redoubtable Italian artillery, however, continued to bombard their Allied counterparts whilst safely well out of range. They could claim they were doing something about the situation. Wadi Derna fell on 30 January. Alan Moorehead found himself accompanied by a Libyan correspondent of an Italian newspaper, who had also decided to surrender.

'No like Itie bangs,' he explained to Moorehead. 'They go crazy. We go to cookhouse now. Itie grub not good. Happy Christmas, sir.'

'Tell him to sod off back to the Ities,' suggested an Aussie soldier.

'No, no,' implored the intrepid correspondent. 'Spaghetti give me the trollops an' all. We go to the cookhouse now, General, sir?'

Moorehead also met another prisoner, who was a lawyer from Rome. They were under fire.

'It's your side firing,' claimed Signor Pugliese, accustomed to disputes.

'It's not,' contended Moorehead. 'It's your lot.'

'Well, I'll tell you what,' suggested Pugliese, 'I'll stand up and then, because it's the British, they will open fire at me. Then you stand up and they'll see that you are British and stop firing.'

'No way will I do that,' refused the *Daily Express* writer.

Later, at Beda Fomm on 5 February, 20,000 more Italians surrendered along with 200 heavy guns and 120 tanks. Amongst the prisoners were, by all accounts, 'a couple of bints'. Apparently, they had been cooking, washing and cleaning for the Italians and saw no reason to discontinue their war services just because it was a different army – just like the prostitute in Sidi Barrani. The full extent of their duties was not clear.

On 6 February the Australians occupied Benghazi and captured seven generals. Some records claim these included Bergonzoli, but, according to Moorehead, 'Old Electric Whiskers', as Bergonzoli was fondly called, could not be found. The mystery deepened.

East Africa

On 19 January 1941 British and South African forces had launched a three-pronged assault towards Addis Ababa, the capital of Ethiopia, which was part of the Italian Empire. The exiled emperor of Ethiopia (Abyssinia), Haile Selassie, visited a wounded South African soldier (known widely as 'Tiger Tim') in hospital on 10 February.

'How do you feel?' asked the concerned emperor.

'Go away, you little black bastard,' responded Tiger Tim.

On the next day Divisional HQ issued a Special General Routine Order. 'In future, His Imperial Majesty, Haile Selassie, King of Kings and Lion of Judah, will not, repeat, will not be referred to as that little black bastard.'

As April arrived, Addis Ababa came under a heavy Allied onslaught. The British commander was attempting to accelerate an already pronounced tendency for Italian soldiers to surrender so he rigged up an enormous loudspeaker to broadcast to the enemy across the valley. Contrary to expert opinion the Italians did not shoot at it. Indeed, as excerpts from Italian opera floated over, the Italians stopped shooting and started singing. There were infrequent interruptions to the music in order to let the enemy know about their latest military disasters. They stopped singing but as soon as the concert resumed so did they.

The city fell on 5 April but occupying Allied troops were not free of trouble from the citizens, who did not care much for any Europeans, Australians or South Africans. They became more of a nuisance than the Italian army. Perhaps they had heard of Tiger Tim's treatment of their emperor. Alan Moorehead's driver, a Londoner, was confused by it all.

''Oo the f***ing 'ell we fighting, anyway?'

Moorehead could not really enlighten him. He went up in a Valencia bomber every day for a while: it was doing communication work. However, the enthusiastic crew became frustrated with this limited role because they flew over a huge Italian fort every day without being able to drop anything on it. They decided on unilateral action, filling up a dustbin with a broken-up sewing machine, old bottles, nails and any old iron and rammed it down with a charge of cordite, attaching a fuse to it.

Excited by their ingenuity, at the first sight of the fort they lit the fuse and prepared to trundle the dustbin over to the bomb hatch. But it weighed at least a proverbial ton, and they failed to shift it despite some rather frantic and desperate heaving. The fuse was getting short. They managed to get it out of the hatch with seconds to spare after Herculean, even maniacal efforts.

The explosion came seconds later and blew the bomber up a 100ft or more. Later news reported the total destruction of the fort and its defenders.

Rommel arrives

Around this time General Rommel arrived in North Africa with an army. One of his enduring problems throughout the North African campaign was getting supplies across the sea, especially petrol. British warships from Malta continually attacked the German convoys. The British vessels themselves faced the gauntlet of enemy submarines. On 16 April HMS *Mohawk* was sunk. Rating Ted Sullivan was picked up by a Carling craft and lit up a desperately needed fag.

'I don't think we should smoke, chaps,' someone warned him cheerfully. 'We might give our position away to the enemy.' The whole area was brightly lit by a raging naval battle so the quip was well received by an intelligent audience.

'I've lost all me money,' complained Ted to all and sundry. 'I was saving it for Carmelita.'

There came more howls of merriment: Carmelita was the star of the red light district in Valetta.

Only a few days later Rommel was in Egypt. Operation Brevity drove him back but he was soon on the advance again and reached as far as General Bergonzoli had the previous year. Bombardier Reg Crimp of the 2nd Battalion of the Rifle Brigade luckily escaped all this hassle, being sent back to Egypt to guard Italian POWs.

This was a doddle compared to the front line: the 'prisoners' were out all day at work. No self-respecting Italian prisoner had any thoughts of escape. In any case, fleeing into the wilds of the Western Desert was not clever. So Reg spent a lot of time at the pictures. This particular establishment was run by an 'Egyptian gentleman' popularly known as 'Shafto'. It cost 3 pias for other ranks and 10 for officers.

Programmes were made up of vintage movies – when the equipment was in working order (even then the screen resembled London in a smog). During frequent breakdowns the jam-packed audience enjoyed much booing and whistling (if the film was bad they enjoyed it even more).

Reg was in reserve near Mersa Matruh guarding the battalion cash box on 5 September. The previous box had been mysteriously stolen so an entire team of guards was on duty. Reg stood on a plank over a hole with the box at the bottom of it. Morale was low because no one had any money to go to Cairo. If the thieves were caught there were threats of a lynching. Cairo was a wild city.

Reg was still guarding in October, this time in Thalatta: he was in charge of the rations along with 'Squirts' Mulbey, an old soldier. 'Squirts' meant bomb happy. He wore a colossal topee (helmet) which rested on his ears and was never removed, even in the shower – a rare occurrence. He spoke a foreign language.

'Taro, China, just shifty this. The koodoo's zift duff scoff peachy if Ombasha can't buddly 'em.'

It was a cocktail of Urdu, Hindu and Arabic plus traces of army and cockney slang. A fair translation of Squirt's point was, 'One moment, pal, just look at this. The whole lot's bad. Rotten meat soon if the corporal can't get it exchanged'.

Tobruk

The Second World War, like the Great War, depended to some extent on tea, or 'char', as an old soldier would call it. As Rommel continued to besiege Tobruk in November 1941, Reg's battalion used up a hundred gallons of petrol a day to brew up. They had more petrol than water. In the city, at the hospital, doctors, nurses and orderlies spent a lot of their time in slit trenches during German bombardments. The colonel was irritated by these shows of cowardice, as he called it. Finally, the third raid in an hour caused him to lose his patience:

'Get back to your work,' he ordered sharply, standing in open ground. 'Look at me, I'm not rushing about like a fool.'

A voice rang out from the trench. 'Neither would we if we were your age, you silly old bastard!'

It was Sergeant Clark, but Colonel Spears didn't bat an eyelid. Clark was his stockbroker in civvy street.

The 2nd Battalion of the Rifle Brigade were bang in the middle of Operation Crusader, designed to push the Germans deeply back into Libya. By 22 November they had had no NAAFI rations for a fortnight, but, even worse, no fags. Squirts and an equally experienced campaigner smoked dried tealeaves wrapped in newspaper.

Meanwhile, the siege of Tobruk raged on: Surgeon Ralph Marnham operated in the hospital round the clock and was on his feet so long his legs swelled up alarmingly. 'Stick a knife in, see what comes out,' suggested a helpful colleague.

In the next theatre a Polish surgeon refused to operate on a wounded German on the grounds that his mortality rate would be 100 per cent.

This was on 7 December 1941. On the same day, John Garcia, a Hawaiian, who lived in Pearl Harbor, was awakened early by his grandmother with the news that the Japanese were attacking.

John was not impressed. 'They're only practising, Granny,' he reassured her.

Syria and Lebanon

Yet another war front began in 1941. On 8 June French troops entered Syria and Lebanon (Operation Exporter) in order to overthrow the Vichy garrison, which would have been able to ease the Wehrmacht's passage to Palestine and the Suez Canal. But the Vichy surrendered on 21 June.

CHEER UP, MATE!

Alan Moorehead and other journalists were called upon to witness the surrender signatures in a big hotel. But all the lights failed and the room was plunged into darkness. Driver Harper was instructed to bring his motorbike upstairs to throw some light on the proceedings.

Having dragged his machine up the palatial staircase Harper kick-started it into life and the room was flooded with brilliant light. However, no one could hear anything above the roar of the engine.

A colonel yelled into Harper's ear: 'Turn the bloody thing off!'

'If I turn it off, sir, you won't have no light.' So he and his bike were dismissed and the diplomats turned to a hurricane lamp and the Suez Canal was saved.

SIX

The Blitz Continued
1941

Even more news from Glasgow

On 4 January Waddell's sausage factory in the city was machine-gunned by German fighters. There was prolonged debate in Pam Ashford's office as to whether the Luftwaffe had intended it as their target. It all depended on your view of Waddell's sausages. To some people, they were God's gift towards the perfect sausage but to others ...

Portsmouth was struck by 50,000 incendiary bombs on the same day and Miss Bousie in Glasgow said that she blamed herself entirely for the war.

'I did not press hard enough for proportional representation,' she explained to Pam Ashworth.

There was some good news on the 11th, however. 'The Italians have given up fish and chips,' announced a bloke on a bus in the city.

'How do you know that?' demanded the conductor.

'They've run out of Greece.'

Pam Ashford was concerned about another item of news – that if the Nazis conquered Britain Nordic-type woman would be selected to be their second wives.

'In that case,' she ruminated, 'I'm booked for an Italian – always wanted to see Venice.' On 9 February she was shocked, amongst many, apparently, at Winston Churchill's blasphemous misuse of

Matthew VII, 7. On the other hand, she was pleased to discover that Lord Haw-Haw had given strict instructions that the Shawlands area of Glasgow should not be attacked because he had an aunty living there.

London early in the year

On 18 January a Free French pilot had a few days leave in London. He stayed in a small hotel. After a nice evening out he went to bed, but in the morning the whole place was deserted. Looking around in some bewilderment he came across a policeman.

'There's an unexploded bomb along the street,' he explained. 'Sorry, sir, we seemed to have missed you out.'

'Will it be moved today?' asked the pilot.

'You are forgetting, sir,' said the copper, 'it is a Sunday today. The bomb squad will be back tomorrow, alright.'

A little later that day the queen was in the Buckingham Palace air-raid shelter with Henry Hopkins, President Roosevelt's emissary. She told him that what counted in the Blitz was the morale and determination of the great mass of Britons. A couple of workmen passed in front of the gates.

'I bet they've got 'eating in their bleedin' shelter,' one complained to his mate.

Meanwhile, in the Tilbury air-raid shelter in Stepney, those crowded inside faced as much danger from criminals and thugs as the Luftwaffe. A policeman chasing a wanted man was beaten up on 4 January and the shelter marshal was knocked senseless by a woman without an entry ticket on 28 January. Next, a thief stole all of Gerrit Beatvelsen's clothes. Gerrit met the felon in the street a few days later, but he was a big bloke and so Gerrit said nothing despite the fact that the devil was wearing his extremely expensive braces.

Heavy bombing over London resumed in March. A friend of mine was trapped in a blazing building.

'What did you do?' I asked him.

'I sang the National Anthem,' he revealed.

'What for?'

'They said I gotta sing an' the only song I knew all the way through was the National Anthem.'

Another young lad wrote home from evacuation: 'They call it Spring, mum. They have it once a year down here'.

Walter Handy, a Wandsworth man, claimed that he was bombed out nineteen times in five months and was sent to prison for three years where he was safer. Looting became rife: one notable ringleader was 7 years old, whilst a part-time ARP Warden was found in possession of 130 pairs of ladies' gloves, 214 towels, seventeen bottles of hair tonic, two fur coats and a fur collar.

The foreman of a demolition squad worked in a house where a bomb blast had knocked every shilling out of the gas meter yet had failed to break a single light bulb.

Meanwhile, the Metropolitan Police continued to do their bit by keeping pigs in Hyde Park (everyone was being exhorted to 'Dig for Victory'). This enterprise had a very high security rating and the BBC were even refused an interview with Inspector Smith, who was in charge of the pigs. His sergeant (disguised as a scarecrow – well, he looked like one, anyway) pushed a barrow of pigswill through Mayfair, but security was so intense that the local bobbie had not been informed about the pigs.

'Hello, hello, hello, there, what we got here, then?'

'You ignorant f***ing c***,' snarled the sergeant, 'can't you see who I am?'

The Home Guard were equally active: the Ministry of Supply had its own unit, practising with Lewis machine guns at Wormwood Scrubs. It was even reported that the ministry's famous and traditional motto, 'If it moves, file it' was now converted to, 'If it moves, shoot it'.

Joan Wyndham left a rather comfortable life as an art student to join the WAAF (Women's Auxiliary Air Force). She had to certify that she had never had fits, never wet the bed and had never suffered from suppuration of the ears, St Vitus Dance or V.D.

Following those declarations, she had to pee into a milk bottle for a doctor whom she suspected of being a lesbian. She hit Joan's knee violently with a rubber hammer and Joan's foot (inadvertently) flew up and collided with the doctor's nose.

Gossip must go on – Blitz or no Blitz. (Reproduced by kind permission of Getty Images)

In retaliation, she stuck tubes in Joan's ears and gave her a stringent eye test. Joan could hardly see the card let alone the letters on it but she had learnt them off by heart whilst waiting.

In April, the night of 16/17 went down in history as 'The Wednesday' as the Luftwaffe made a desperate attempt to kill as many civilians as they could and disrupt the lives of countless others. In Cheyne Walk, Chelsea, an ambulance driver, June Spencer, went to the aid of a bomb blast victim. An enormous special constable, sporting a fabulous, bushy black beard, was crouched over a large plane of glass lying flat on the pavement. It moved, and from underneath crawled Stanley Grumm, a well-known local artist. He did not seem to be hurt in any way but was seriously drunk.

'I've got no legs,' he muttered to June.

'You're standing on them,' June pointed out, and they linked arms and danced off merrily down the street in celebration.

A vicar diversifies during the Blitz.

Nearby, in Tite Street, a house where two lady fire-fighters lived was badly damaged. Yet duty called. They had no front door or windows so they took the tin containing the housekeeping money and Dana's new pair of suspender belts, which they didn't want looted when they left the house for work. They couldn't find their helmets, so Dana stuck a saucepan on her head and Naidra donned a frying pan. As they arrived at their place of duty they quickly received their instructions:

'This way, saucepan.'

'Frying pan – over here.'

Elsewhere, the popular 'Stiffs Express' from Waterloo to Brookwood Cemetery was shut down in April due to bomb damage. Even the dead were suffering.

Around the country

April had opened up with the great news that 26,000 boxes of oranges had arrived in Ipswich, providing one orange per person in the town; the basic rate of income tax was 50 per cent; and the last tower at Crystal Palace was demolished to prevent it being used as a marker by the Luftwaffe.

The news was not so good in Southampton. A notice in a shop window announced:

> We regret we are unable to supply: vacuum flasks, saccharine, lipstick, rouges, all types of vanishing cream, all barley sugar sweets, rolls razors and blades, Gillette 7 o'clock razor blades, brushless shaving soap and Nivea cream – until this notice is removed.

Mothers and children fled from Manchester during the April raids. During the fateful raid of 16 April a matriarch insisted on carrying off her pet goldfish, rendering her incapable of taking anything else.

The latest technique of the Luftwaffe was land mines dropped on parachutes, causing extensive lateral damage. Some fell on Cubitt Town so I was still very glad to be in Carmarthenshire, especially as we had been moved from ancient Mrs Jones at Nantgaredig in the valley to young, lively Mrs Jones in a modern farm up on the hill at Capel Duwy. Here, I was really able to learn the joys of rural existence – being chased by geese, that sort of experience. I was learning Welsh in the village school and by the end of April I could say '*Nos star*', which I believe means 'Goodnight'.

A terrible May

On 10 May 500 bombers attacked London, dropping a large number of land mines and causing the destruction of 5,000 houses. Vera Reid recalled that a man near her laughed uproariously in the thick of the onslaught as he surveyed scenes of utter devastation.

'My heart,' she wrote in her diary, 'melted with love for him and everyone.'

The one good thing about this raid was that it proved to be the last of the Blitz. London had the largest loss of life on 10 May than on any other single night – 1,436. Fires raged from Romford to Hammersmith. A third of the capital's streets became impassable and 15,000 people were left without gas or electricity. The Royal College of Surgeons was badly damaged but the skeleton of the infamous Irish thief, Charles Byrne, all 7ft of it, was saved for posterity. Private hotels in the Vauxhall Bridge Road were destroyed but, owing to the fact that these were the haunts of prostitutes, it proved impossible to compile the names and addresses of all victims.

Lipton's warehouse in the City Road was also hit, providing an intoxicating aroma of good coffee. In fact, infused coffee poured out of the building and firemen pumped it back in again – fire-fighting with café espresso.

A lady of the night was still gallantly on duty in Piccadilly as incendiaries rained down. Gaily, she put up her umbrella and sang, 'I'm singing in the rain, just singing in the rain'.

In 'War Weapons Week', volunteers were sought to organise Bring and Buy stalls to raise money for the war effort. One such organiser was Nella Last, an M.O. diarist. She reported that Thursday 13 May was especially fruitful at the local WVS meeting, mainly due to Nella's hard work. However, the rather superior Mrs Lord was irritated by Nella's enterprise since it was she who usually did the organising. She voiced her displeasure.

'Sh, sh, sh – not in front of the children,' urged the spiky Nella, and all the 'children', not one under 50, howled with glee. Mrs Lord looked suitably flustered but still tried to make her contribution.

'So little amuses in these hysterical times,' she mused through pursed lips and sent the children into hysterics.

There was hardly a night in May when one city or another was not attacked. 'Believe me,' Churchill announced to a suffering nation, 'Herr Hitler has his problems, too.'

Hitchhiking became very popular. 'Say, old man, I'm Golders Green.' 'Say, boys, I'm sweet – what about a seat?' were examples of notices hung round hopeful necks. Notices also appeared in shops and stalls: 'More open than usual'. 'We got our oranges from Mussolini's lake' (a reference to one of El Duce's claims).

The message on the fruit stall reads 'Hitler's Bombs can't beat us. Our oranges came through Musso's "lake".' (Reproduced by kind permission of Getty Images)

George Golder, a householder in Silvertown, was bombed out and lived in the brick shelter in his street. He returned home occasionally to try and devise something to eat, despite having no gas, electricity or water. On 23 May he salvaged some bacon and lit a fire in his garden.

As the bacon began to sizzle his landlord came by and asked about the rent. George's reply consisted of only two words.

Gladys Strelitz was also homeless, in East Ham. She had no power but she did have a candle. She built a fire with bricks, paper, bracken and wood and attempted to prepare porridge and sausages.

'When will it be ready, mummy?' asked little Jane eagerly.

'You can't 'urry nothing up, love,' explained Gladys patiently. 'It's ready when it's ready and not before.' Such was the Blitz spirit.

Repartee in a Plymouth pub was reported:

'Where's the gents, mate?'

'Everywhere's the gents now, mate.'

In a nearby large public shelter Mr Churchill and Lady Astor were trying to raise spirits: she turned unlikely cartwheels to cheer everybody up.

Despite the fury of the late Blitz, the London war industry was flourishing. The new Mosquito bomber was being mass-produced in Walthamstow. It was made of many sheets of plywood and balsa wood stuck together. This was as tough as metal but much lighter so the Mosquito was fast, especially after a good wax with furniture polish.

Meanwhile, in a cellar under the House of Commons, they were building submarines. It was staffed by relations of MPs, secretaries, legal advisers, policemen, postmen and firemen. Everyone looked the same – in large white overalls.

The 'Norwegian Camel Corps' was doing a marvellous job on unexploded bombs after extensive training by the Royal Engineers. The 'NCC' was really the 'Non-Combatant Corps' – made up of conscientious objectors, or 'conchies'.

SEVEN

Later In 1941

Foreign affairs in May

Rudolf Hess, the deputy Nazi leader and one of Hitler's problems, dropped in on Eaglesham in Scotland by parachute. There ensued widespread agreement amongst the Allies and Nazis that Hess was nuts.

The Nazi leader now had designs on Russia and moved armies and bombers to the East. Meanwhile, British forces were trying to hold on in Greece and Crete and also deal with the Iraqis, who were thinking of throwing in their lot with the Germans. The main concern of Britain in Iraq was reliance on the Arab Legion and the Transjordan Frontier Force. Would they fight?

'The Arab Legion will fight anybody,' their commander, Major-General Glubb, declared. That was what General Wilson, the British commander in Palestine, was worried about.

Summer

On 1 June clothes rationing began in Britain and a culture of scruffiness developed around this legitimate excuse. You could Dig for Victory, Bring and Buy for Victory or simply put two fingers up in a 'V' salute at every opportunity for Victory.

Also, as part of the drive for victory, women aged between nineteen and forty had to register for war work. Muriel Green, another Mass Observationist, had volunteered long before that and travelled all over Britain helping out at various hostels – cooking, gardening, cleaning, etc. She worked in Dorset, Rutland, Suffolk, Gloucester, Taunton and elsewhere. She was typical of a hard-working, tough, rather merry band of itinerant young women, not averse to having a good time during the few hours they had off work. On 1 July Muriel arranged to meet two airmen. Her excuse was that she was 'mass-observing the forces' love affairs'.

As the war shifted to Russia and then further east to the Pacific, mass bombing became more likely in Moscow or Leningrad or Pearl Harbor, rather than the Isle of Dogs. But there were still enough Jerry planes to create a nuisance over British cities. Liverpool was kept out of bed for the whole night of 23 July. Censorship being what it was, the *Liverpool Echo* reported the next morning that 'Many ack-ack guns have been in action over a north-west town', as if its bleary-eyed readers needed reminding.

On 27 July a bomb lodged in a gutter in a house in Canning Town and caused next door's electricity meter to race away. The Electricity Board still demanded what was on the clock, even though the bill was enough for the whole street. The hapless householder applied to the local Assistance Board for compensation but was turned down on the grounds that the bomb was 'An Act of God' (rather than 'An Act of Herman Goering'). Then the householder tried the Legal Aid Board but they decided she did not qualify for legal assistance. Community spirit saved the day: there was a whip-round in the street.

Assistance Boards were kept very busy, what with land mines and incendiaries. One notable case concerned a soldier whose wife ran off and took all her daughter's clothes with her. The Board provided the money for new clothes but then the wife returned. She then cleared off again, stealing all the new clothes ... and so it went on.

Pam Ashford's colleague, the vociferous Miss Bousie, announced a 'sensation' on 30 July. 'Hitler and Goering have quarrelled,' she said with baited breath (which was actually quite prophetic).

Miss Ashford was unmoved: 'Tell me that Goering has shot Hitler and committed suicide – that would be a sensation.'

Home Guard still on its toes

Despite the fading fears of invasion the Home Guard remained on full alert. On 8 August Charles Grove took part in exercises in Regent's Park during which he had to pretend that he was a German parachutist by waving an umbrella about for three hours. Meanwhile, fellow Home Guards rushed hither and thither in order to practise what they would do if Charles had been a real invader. He was a reporter for the *Daily Mail* and the *Sunday Express*, a novelist and a busy socialite.

On 15 August he was back in the park dressed up properly as a member of the German army. Later in the evening he was at the Savoy for supper.

The BBC Home Guard was now on top of its game. Anyone entering the building had to produce an official pass. On 9 August several employees gained access using passes signed 'Adolf Hitler', 'Stanley Baldwin' and 'Marlene Dietrich', the latter enabling a bald and short-sighted technician to gain entrance.

Commissionaires (to a man, old soldiers) trained senior BBC executives in the use of rifles and the latter made a point of saluting the doormen with their rolled umbrellas whenever entering Portland House.

Famously, the Home Guard became armed with 'Lord Croft's Pikes' in October (Croft was the junior minister credited with this bold plan). The War Office defended this move with the assertion that pikes were lethal in hand-to-hand fighting in the streets.

Other lethal weapons were brought to bear. One officer was alarmed to find one of his men armed with rotten potatoes containing razor blades. The major suggested that someone might get seriously hurt.

'Not them, mister,' insisted the man, 'it 'ud just bounce off them bastards.'

It is thus no surprise to discover that private property meant little to the brave souls ready to face the Hun. On 7 September Swanley Cricket Club were attempting to play a match when a horde of 'German paratroopers' swept across the field, trampling the pitch and causing several dents on a good length.

Swanley and Orpington Home Guard invade the cricket pitch, 7 September 1941.

The players had only just recovered from this onslaught when back the 'paratroopers' came, hotly pursued by imitation tanks and bazookas.

Now that the Blitz was over (and I was back home) ack-ack batteries presented a formidable defence barrier. The one on the Isle of Dogs located on the 'Mudchute' (a raised central area made with the spoil from digging out the docks) was highly reassuring. The noise from each gun was quite individual. It was easy to identify the 'pop-pop', the 'tennis raquet', the 'wang-wang' and the 'plop-plop'. Fired together they made a fearful noise, and one which cracked our toilet seat on three occasions, splintered our front door and knocked my dad over on another.

The science of bomb-dodging was now highly sophisticated: one theory was that the same building was never hit twice, but there was no real rush to test it out.

Problems in the Third Reich

As Mr Churchill kept reminding us, Hitler had his own problems. However, he did not hold a monopoly over troubles in the Third Reich:

Friedrich Reck-Malleczewen, a member of the Bavarian aristocracy, reported buying a pair of ski shoes which fell apart after just half an hour on the slopes.

They were made of cardboard.

More seriously, the pulpy bread being sold to the citizens of Munich was causing widespread and foul breaking of wind from bottoms. Reck-Malleczewen described the atmosphere in the cafés as 'pestilential'. He also complained about wine which tasted like 'unholy snake poison'. Berlin was no healthier: a curious pong hung over the city like a venomous cloud.

When the German Field Pastor Sebacher reached the Russian front on 5 December he was glad of temperatures of minus -30°C because it killed off the hundreds of lice and nits which had travelled with him.

Trouble was also emerging from Tampere in Finland where a dog named Jackie, owned by Tor Borg, was given the nickname 'Hitler' because of his habit of giving Nazi salutes, paw held high in the air. This could not be allowed to go on and on 29 January 1941 Willy Erkelenz, the German vice-consul in Helsinki, summoned Tor to the German embassy to answer serious questions about his dog. Tor blamed it all on his wife, Josefine (who was actually German – which

made the misbehaviour even worse). Erkelenz sent a detailed report to Berlin but the authorities could not nail Tor because witnesses who said they saw Hitler, sorry, Jackie, being disrespectful refused to come forward.

Jackie, in sunglasses, with Tor Borg. (Associated Press)

Black market

Maggie Joy Blunt, a Mass Observationist, wrote on 21 September that her greengrocer had slipped her two oranges from under the counter:

'But don't think for a moment that the war is over,' he declaimed solemnly.

During October, 150,000 eggs could be found 'off the ration' at a penny each in Bradford. In the same month 80,000 ration books were stolen from the Brighton Food Office. Undercover officers (or 'snoopers') were offered shoals of them at a good price. The trail finally led back to the ringleader of the scam, a female ration enforcement officer working in the Food Office who had initially reported the theft. She got three years.

In fact, the law was kept very busy on the Home Front. Mr Justice Charles opened the Lewes Assizes on 1 December by declaring that all but five cases in the coming calendar featured service personnel – with bigamy, housebreaking and rape well to the fore. In all such cases, he claimed, he would be told that the servicemen and servicewomen involved were excellent soldiers, sailors or air crew. Bigamy was back in fashion because possessing two or three wives meant you could claim multiple marriage allowances.

Women at work

With women being directed into war work even their children had to muck in. Amy Briggs's young daughter was thus called upon to prepare the family tea (early evening meal) for the first time in her life on 31 October. She cut the bread into slices at least 2in thick and smothered them with the family's jam ration for a week. She also had the fire blazing half-way up the chimney, threatening to set the whole house alight.

Amy was a nurse in Leeds. Having her home nearly burnt down was bad enough but even worse was the news that her husband, Ted, had a week's leave from the army. As soon as he arrived he went straight into his usual tirade, accusing her of all types of wanton behaviour. When she got rid of him at the end of a dreadful seven days she considered perpetrating some of the misdeeds of which he had accused her.

Nella Last, in the Barrow-in-Furness WVS canteen, had experience of women coming out to work for the first time. There were the 'I'll drop in and do a bit but can't wash up because I've got nail varnish on', and the 'I've forgotten my overall and must not mess up my skirt by going near the stove'.

On 12 December the lads from the local ack-ack battery arrived at the canteen at 3.30 p.m. Even though they had had dinner (lunch) they were famished already. One of the gunners resembled a famous film star.

'Are you related?' asked a hopeful young volunteer.

'Nay,' responded the handsome fellow drolly. 'But I lived in the next village and my father had a bike.'

Mrs Hamer, an older and more serious lady, leaned over the counter and scolded, 'It's not a matter for joking, that,' and the gunners and less humourless volunteers collapsed into jollity.

Another gunner ordered nine slices of toast, a tin opener and a fork.

'What about a toothpick?' suggested Nella.

'Nay, missus, with a tin o' sardines mashed on nine pieces o' toast t' bones 'll not have a chance to stick in teeth nor anywhere else.'

Nella was a fine example of the sturdy and cheerful women who kept the Home Front going. As well as running a family she worked for the WVS and also later opened a Red Cross shop to collect for POWs in Germany.

Married women with young children could volunteer to work, like Nella. Joan Collins, a teacher in Ely, worked on her dad's farm and discovered that his cows only delivered when you sang *Santa Lucia* to them, the result of being tended by Italian POWs.

The Blitz now faded from folk memory: Edward Stebbing, another Mass Observationist, reported on 19 October that he had encountered 'that rare creature': a man who always carried around his gas mask and his steel helmet. He was not taking any chances, perhaps he could see into the future.

EIGHT

On Land, Sea and Air 1941

Preparing for service overseas

British soldiers served on many overseas fronts in 1941 – North Africa, Syria, Lebanon, Greece, Crete and Iraq – and there were also the garrisons in the Far East, called into action at the end of the year. Even more fronts were likely to open up in 1942. 56 Heavy Regiment, Royal Artillery, had various detachments in Sussex, including a gun crew in Alfriston. They were billeted in an old inn – upstairs for other ranks, down below for officers.

At one end in the upper storey was 'The Great Gun Bucket', for use during inclement weather but also used frequently by inebriated gunners. Consequently, there was spillage and the ancient floor timbers began to rot. One fateful night the whole caboodle fell through the floor on to Lieutenant Sebag-Montifiore, sleeping peacefully below – the ceiling, the Great Gun Bucket and 20 gallons of well-matured urine.

It all subsequently blew over, but it was generally hoped that the brave lieutenant would get a posting overseas – and the sooner the better.

Bombing Germany

Throughout November and December 1940 British bombers attacked German cities. On 8 November Hitler had to run for shelter instead of strutting around a stage delivering his annual 'State of the Nation' speech. Of 125,000 British bomber crew in the war 55,573 were killed (44 per cent).

In their few hours off bombers tried to relax by enjoying themselves as much as they could. It was on the bike or bus to the nearest or best pub (fighter pilots travelled by car). Flight Sergeant Jackie Hole was known as 'Lover Boy' because of his reputation for going with any woman – ugly, fat, skinny, whatever. They often wondered how he managed in the very worst cases.

'You don't look at the fireplace,' he explained laconically, 'when you're poking the fire.'

There were Aussies at Kidlington and their favourite trick was to put Sergeant O'Reilly (son of the famous spin bowler) up against a wall and fire darts at his large, protruding ears. The Mass Observationist at the base, Flight Lieutenant George Bell, could only watch this ritual when he was blind drunk.

Between 14 and 23 July 1941 bombers delivered half the tonnage of bombs dropped by the Luftwaffe on London to date in the war. A film was issued at the end of this period featuring a real raid and a real pilot – Squadron Leader Pickard. It was called *Target for Tonight* and this became a catchphrase on radio and stage. At least it was more optimistic than the earlier catchphrase, 'Don't you know there's a war on'.

Fighters

Fighter Command was also sending Spitfires and Hurricanes to raid commerce and industry in France (a Hurricane bomber was developed). The Free French were very disappointed that they were not allowed to take part, mainly because of the fear that if they were captured their families, still in France, would be threatened unless the pilots divulged vital information. René Mouchotte's mother was still in Oran, North Africa. Fighter Command finally relented and Mouchotte completed 141 sweeps before he was shot down and killed.

Fighter pilots, of course, were just as mad as their bomber counterparts. Mouchotte had difficulty in discovering what was comic about some of their exploits. At Drem Airfield in Scotland he remembered the enormous copper goblet which stood in the fireplace of the mess. Once or twice a week this was filled with 20 pints of ale and some unfortunate airman was expected to drink the lot, after which they carried him off unconscious. Mouchotte did not get the joke; neither, he suspected, did the victim.

The Free French got their own squadrons later in 1941 but Mouchotte's description of the planes provided for them was 'tin cans', or 'flat irons' (his English was improving). Edinburgh he found eternally gloomy, made worse by the atrocious weather and the blackout. He was cheered up by the delivery of a blue, very thick, hand-knitted sweater – that is, until he tried it on. However, he got a nice letter and photograph with it and the knitter looked young and pretty. Indeed, he hoped to meet her. Some further light relief was provided by General de Gaulle's special representative, a woman with a moustache enthusiastically trying to devise leisure and comfort for the pilots – but she was neither young nor pretty.

The French did have difficulty getting in touch with their loved ones. A comrade of Mouchotte's sent a letter to France on 10 October and it was opened by the censor, who scribbled across it in red ink: 'The swine of a censor has opened your letter and read it but he has let it pass all the same.'

Pilot Officer W. Cunningham of 19 Squadron (Spitfires) was shot down near Amsterdam after taking part in a raid on Cologne in August. A novice machine-gunner claimed the hit but Cunningham refused to be shot down by any Tom, Dick or Harry.

'Horsecock!' he scoffed. 'No bloody machine gunner could shoot me down. It was the ships in the estuary. Horsecock!'

He was not a happy pilot. Apart from being shot down he had an abscess on his backside and a sty on his eye.

At sea

On 27 March 1941 the Battle of Matapan, south of Crete, more or less eliminated the Italian navy in the Mediterranean, which Mussolini had described as 'an Italian Lake'. But the tonnage of merchant ships being lost to U-boat action in the Atlantic (31,000 tons just in four days in April) was a serious threat to the British economy.

On 24 May HMS *Hood* was sunk by the *Bismarck* just off the coast of Greenland. Able Seaman Bob Tilburn on *Hood* vividly remembered his captain, 'Hooky' Walter, who had lost his left hand in an accident. He wore a silver hook during weekdays and a gold one on Sundays.

Bob was one of the very few who survived the *Hood* sinking – three out of 1,418. He was rescued by the destroyer *Electra*. The captain of this vessel said to Bob that he could accompany them in the imminent assault on the *Bismarck* or he could go to hospital. HMS *Hood* had 15in armour plating; *Electra* had 0.5in armour plating. Bob went to hospital.

As he entered the ward a bloke called out to him: 'Hey, sailor, it's just been on the radio, did you know the Hood's been sunk?'

Bob's response was terse, and personal.

But on 27 May *Electra* was one of the ring of warships which disposed of the *Bismarck*. Dick Harrell can remember that day vividly. He was not on a warship but in school in Manchester. When the news came through his class were having a music lesson.

'Open the doors and windows, Harrell,' the music teacher commanded. Harrell did as he was told.

'Now, children,' continued the teacher, 'we will sing "Rule Britannia".' And they did, very loudly.

As the glorious phrase 'Britain never, never will be slaves' echoed away Harrell was ordered to close the doors and windows. And he obeyed once more.

On the day after Pearl Harbor HMS *Prince of Wales* was torpedoed by Japanese bombers off Malaya and the order to abandon ship was given.

Able Seaman Ted Neville called out to his closest pal: 'Come on, jump, mate. Cheer up, mate, because all them bleedin' explosions have frightened off the bleedin' sharks.'

There was now better news from the Atlantic. In a six-day battle in December four of nine U-boats were destroyed and only one merchant ship out of thirty-two. Furthermore, on 28 December, British commandoes raided the German naval base in Maloy in Norway and the tidings interrupted Hitler at dinner and gave him indigestion.

NINE

North Africa 1942

Cairo

The end of 1941 had seen Rommel driven back by Operation Crusader to the point where he had set out eight months before. But the New Year witnessed changing fortunes in this seesaw war. Cyrenaica once again fell to the Afrika Corps. Bombardier Reg Crimp was lucky to get leave in Cairo at the end of January.

Reg and his chum, Arthur Grace, were immediately engulfed by the locals flourishing well-soiled cards under their noses recommending 'chosen hotels'. They eventually arrived in a near-derelict building. However, other soldiers seemed happy there so they stayed.

There were new experiences for the lads: single deck trams with scores of 'buckshee' passengers hanging on by their fingertips, and horse-drawn gharries providing a faint but all-pervading whiff of horse dung, like Berlin.

Crimp and Grace were served watery beer in a 'dance hall', where plain 'bints' cadged drinks but kept well clear of exploratory military hands. The sex-starved troops grew frustrated and started throwing bottles and shooting at the chandeliers. The MPs arrived. But the night soon came to an end – even the whorehouses closed at 10 p.m. sharp.

Alan Moorehead was also in the city in February with fellow reporters. At Central Station a group of 'porters' leapt into their taxi, grabbed their bags and tore off into the murky depths of the thronging terminus. Richard Dimbleby went to get tickets and Moorehead went in search of their bags. As they struggled forward through the mob persistent vendors offered them water, 'whisky', sticks, pornography, tiny glasses containing a mysterious yellow syrup, lottery tickets, mutilated bars of chocolate and booklets on how to avoid paying taxes.

Rommel again

As Rommel re-approached Egypt, threatening Tobruk, Reg Crimp found himself engaged in endless exercises at Sollum which he described as 'a load of bollocks'. However, he was kept entertained by a comrade known as 'Mo' Cabbett, 'Mo' being short for 'Mohammed'. Cabbett fancied himself as a Muslim and was immersing himself in the language and religion. This did not prevent him from maintaining a hot and intimate correspondence with 'a lady in England' and simultaneously considering settling down with 'a bint from the Berka' (brothel).

Moorehead was in Tobruk in June 1942 when Rommel's heavy artillery was pummelling the city. This caused problems with parking since cars were an attractive target for the enemy artillery. The correspondents chose the Y.M.C.A building as a safe option.

'You can't park 'ere, mate,' a corporal informed them in time-honoured fashion. 'They think it's important if you park cars outside it.'

They eventually chose a mosque which had been re-named 'Red Lion – Free Beer Tomorrow'.

Tobruk fell on 28 June and Bert Fisher waited in his slit trench outside the town for Rommel. He did not fancy his chances with a rifle against a Tiger tank. Everybody was very nervous, especially the lorry driver waiting by Bert's trench for orders. Quite suddenly, a bren gun carrier came hurtling up the track. The trouble with desert warfare was that you never knew who or where anybody was. The driver was fairly confident about Bert being British because of some lusty Anglo-Saxon, but whose side the gun carrier was on was anybody's guess. He made up his mind.

'F***ing Jerry,' he yelled out and jumped into Bert's trench.

'He speaks f***ing good English,' Bert pointed out, squirming in his trench to get comfortable. It was only designed to take one person.

'They do, don't they, the f***ing Jerries,' insisted the driver. 'But he's got a funny accent.'

'He's a f***ing New Zealander, that's why,' said Bert.

The next month, July, witnessed rapidly changing fortunes: Rommel was halted at El Alamein but Cairo was still under threat. The Allies fought back but Crimp was stranded in Cairo due to transport problems. By the time he did get back to his unit on 10 July the battle for Raweisat Ridge was under way.

'You want your f***ing brains tested, china,' observed a chum. 'Fancy coming back when it's getting heavy. Couldn't you scrounge a cushy job in Cairo? Jerry's on three sides of us here.'

It was all very alarming. General Auchenlech moved his HQ to Cairo in a tented site by the city. It was soon christened by ironic troops 'The Short Range Desert Group', a parody of the 'Long Range Desert Group', tip-top troops on special missions.

In the Med

The war at sea in the Mediterranean was crucial for both sides – getting supplies through to the Battle of Malta. On 13 August Captain Dudley Mason, running the gauntlet of U-boats with his convoy to Malta, was under air attack, too. He had a call from his chief officer.

'A Stuka bomber has bounced off the sea onto the poop,' he said.

'That's nothing,' retorted the captain, 'we've had a Junkers 88 on the foredeck for half an hour.'

He wasn't kidding: two marauding enemy bombers were on board in half an hour.

El Alamein

On 25 August the 1st Battalion of the Rifle Brigade was fighting Rommel on the Alun Halfa Ridge. A rifleman was captured by a Tiger tank and the commander spoke from his turret.

'Uhr,' he called, pointing to his wrist.

'Half past six,' responded the new prisoner of war.

'Nein, nein,' said the commander in irritation. A prisoner's watch was the first spoil of war, even before the rifle.

Rommel attacked on 30 August but the de-coders at Bletchley Park were aware of his plans and also how short he was on petrol because of severe losses of his supply ships. He was now confronted with General Montgomery, a different proposition from the likes of Major-General Messervy, an infantryman commanding an armoured division, and 'a silly old man from the Indian Army who had never seen a tank before and who was so slow he was captured on his first serious day in the desert', according to Sergeant Jake Wardrop of the 5th Royal Tank Regiment.

The assault on Tobruk on 13 September by the Allies failed with heavy losses, however. Chief Engine-Room Officer Trevor Lewis had to jump overboard from HMS *Sikh*. He and other wounded survivors clung to Carley floats.

'Where's the bloody taxi I ordered?' Trevor called out.

Montgomery made thorough preparations for the coming battle at El Alamein by closing all the whorehouses in Cairo, leaving nothing to chance. Between El Alamein and the Quattara Depression dummy tanks, guns and vehicles were assembled for several weeks in the battle zone and then replaced by real ones a few days before the battle. In the southern sector there were dummy unfinished pipelines. Dummy supplies and vehicles were also placed around to give the impression that the battle would start in November, rather than October.

On 14 October the 'Boston Bus Service' commenced – waves of bombers attacking enemy lines. The battle began in the last week of the month and raged for five days. On 28 October Jerry tanks were being knocked out in their dozens by Reg Crimp's battalion, and his CO and adjutant borrowed rifles to pick off the crews escaping from the stricken Tigers. They kept the score as if they were out shooting grouse.

A bedraggled Italian tried to surrender to Reg. 'Tedeschi, no bono,' he claimed in a high-pitched scream as bullets ripped around his feet. 'Mussolini no bono. Me Inglese molto bone.'

By 31 October it was nearly all over and Corporal John Green, a military policeman, celebrated with bacon, beans and Stuka for breakfast. The enemy was now, once again, in headlong retreat towards Libya.

Tunisia

On 8 November the largest amphibious landing force in the history of warfare landed in French North Africa. By 11 November 1,300 miles of coastline were in Allied hands. On 12 November British troops landed in Bone and the battle for Tunisia was won.

Alan Moorehead was in the front line with the Lincolnshire Regiment. He bedded down by some mortars.

'What shall we do if they come over the ridge, sir?' a mortarman asked his officer.

'You'll have to dart around in the bushes,' explained 2nd Lieutenant John Clarke of the Lincolnshire Regiment. The 'bushes' consisted of a few stunted trees almost bare of vegetation.

'F***ing cowboys and Indians,' muttered the soldier glumly. 'Here, sir,' he addressed the war correspondent, 'we've been living on boiled sweets for a week.'

But Moorehead was able later to report that a sack of spuds arrived for the beleaguered troops and that the mortarmen had a difficult night (he did not specify why in the *Daily Express*).

John Clark was, in fact, good at poetry. The following effort was penned during the Tunisian campaign:

> We stumbled down the goat track: thud of boot.
> A belch, a fart and f**k the f***ing anti-tanks!
> Let's see if the Company has left some loot.
> We crawled into their dug-out, struck a match and found
> Three bottles full of whisky, wrapped in tissue paper still.
> The f***ing Jerries won't get this,
> We swigged it as we walked down the road.

Private Ted Smith of the Army Catering Corps was bringing his expertise to the desert. He had the patent for the Mark 1 Desert Stove. This consisted of a trench 12ft long and lined with rows of old biscuit tins filled with water. Timber between the tins was saturated with high-octane petrol. Tins of bully beef, bacon, beans and soya sausages were placed on top of the timbers. More water was poured on them.

When all was ready Ted fired a bullet into the petrol-saturated wood. Boom! Boom! It was breakfast and tea for a whole battalion and the denizens of the nearby village were screaming, 'Allemagne! Allemagne! Bomb-bombs!' and their dogs were going crazy.

Comrades were making tracks for Bone but Ted claimed that he had no need of the official military brothel on account of him being very good looking and also in charge of large quantities of food and drink. Comfortably billeted in the Café Continental in the town he made contact with two rather mysterious Bedouin ladies, obviously captivated by Ted's charms. His theory about his attractiveness looked correct.

They led him back to quite a nice flat and removed their robes and yashmaks: under these they were wearing smart European clothes. Things were getting quite interesting when some Arab men burst through the front door. Ted, always on his toes, grabbed his trousers and scooted out pursued by Arabs, a mob of kids and dogs. There were always dogs. He escaped, to the delight of comrades waiting for their dinners back in camp. The North African campaign was back on course.

Elsewhere 1942

Over there

The year 1942 looked as though it was going to be very different from 1941: the USA was in and it was truly a world war. Breckinridge Long in the State Department in Washington had a vivid recall of 11 December 1941 when Germany and Italy declared war on the USA and the USA declared war on them. It was only four days after Pearl Harbor. 'Hectic!' was Long's verdict.

John Garcia, who was living in Pearl Harbor at the time, later joined the American forces. It was quite a sacrifice because he was earning $128 a week as a shop fitter and in the army he was going to get $21 a month. Others, of course, made even bigger sacrifices: Clark Gable exchanged $357,000 a year for $600 in the 351st Bomber Group at Polebrook in Northamptonshire – a bit different from Hollywood.

During recruitment Garcia was asked about his race but Hawaiians never questioned a person's race. He said that his great-grandparents were from Spain and Wales.

'You're Caucasian, then?' decided the recruiting officer.

'What's that?' wondered John.

'You're white.'

He looked at his dark skin. 'You're kidding,' he said.

Fellow recruits warned him off talking to a group of Jews. 'What's a Jew?' he enquired innocently.

'They killed Jesus.'

'They don't look old enough.'

Elliot Johnson also joined up after Pearl Harbor. One of his friends was half an inch too short for the army so he stayed in bed for four days and even stretched out on the back seat of his mother's car on the journey to the recruiting office. He had grown half an inch.

Over here

The first American soldiers in Britain reached Belfast on 26 January 1942 after the USA had only been in the war for forty-six days. We all know the verdict – 'overpaid, oversexed and over here'. Not so well known is the American verdict on the Tommies – 'under-paid, under-fed, under-sexed and under Eisenhower'.

Officially, the first American soldier to step ashore was Private First Class Milburn H. Henke of the 34th US Infantry Division. His photo was in all the papers the next morning and he received sackfuls of fan mail. *The Times*, more soberly, pointed out that he was the son of a German immigrant. Unfortunately, 500 American soldiers had already docked unnoticed.

'Pearl Harbor? Where's that?' asked kids over here.

'Place in Hawaii,' answered those in the know in a superior fashion.

'Where's that?'

'Dunno. But it's been bombed.'

The GIs (Government Issue – also applied to rubbish and supplies, including toilet paper, but the name stuck, rather like 'Tommy') got lots of advice about being in Britain. Such as: 'Flies spread disease, keep yours

Over here – Private John Ziaja, newly arrived from Adams, Massachusetts, 1942.

'Don't ask foolish questions. Th' schedule calls fer calisthenics. We'll start wid the right eyelid.' (Copyright by Bill Mauldin (1943). Courtesy of the Bill Mauldin Estate LLC)

buttoned'. Cowboys from Texas were put into engineering companies and clerks from New York were placed in the cavalry. The watchword of the American army was adaptability.

They quickly had to adapt to the predilections of this strange country, such as 'Kingston Black', a cider served in the Ostrich pub on the quayside at Bristol. During its maturing the liquor had a lump of (dead) rabbit floating in it to give it body. It was served without the meat but in comparison Al Capone's prohibition rotgut was like distilled water. When GIs stood up after taking some of this brew they discovered that their feet had disappeared.

They didn't like the warm beer, but drank plenty of it nonetheless. In fact, they drank some pubs dry which had not suffered such a cruel fate for centuries. Mostly, they had surprising resilience to British drinks. A GI at Thurleigh, near Bedford, was able to leap onto a bike after many pints but didn't have a clue how to ride when cold sober.

There were language difficulties: a GI wanted an ATS (Auxiliary Territorial Service) girl to pose for a picture under a notice in Norfolk which read: 'Navigation on this Broad is free.' She naturally refused.

'You're through,' telephone operators informed Americans, to whom this phrase meant something entirely different.

Hong Kong falls

In Hong Kong a dirty and tired Canadian soldier, Georges Verrault, led lusty and brave singing on Christmas Day 1941, including the well-favoured song:

Cheer up, mates, bless 'em all,
The long and the short and the tall.
You'll get no promotion
This side of the ocean,
So, cheer up, mates, bless 'em all.

But it was only the short ones they had to worry about; the island surrendered on that day, and the Allies were driven out of Burma by the end of February and later withdrew into Assam.

Advice for airmen

The RAF resumed their raids on France, the Low Countries and Germany. Advice on the mess wall at 615 Squadron at Northolt recommended zig-zagging when faced by enemy ack-ack.

'Above all, arrange matters so that you are always in the zag when he fires at you in the zig, or in the zig when he fires in the zag.'

Elsewhere, Sergeant Pilot Robin Murray was shot down off the Dutch coast on 12 February and injured. His captors put him on a train dressed in pyjamas and a greatcoat. When the train pulled into the station at Breda his German guard spotted some friends on the platform and got off to speak to them. Sergeant Murray hopped out behind him on his crutches and sat on a bench. Then the guard jumped back on and off went the train, leaving his prisoner having a quiet smoke and chatting up some nice Dutch girls.

The train travelled about 300m and then ground to a sudden halt and returned to the station, where the Dutch were having a good laugh at the Jerry's expense. There was also some banter from his mates: 'You will get the Iron Cross from the Führer,' quipped one.

Later, Murray was interrogated by an officer, who told him: 'Don't worry, Sergeant, you will be a prisoner of war for about three years, then you will win the war but unless you get the Poles to negotiate the peace, you'll never win the peace.'

Meanwhile, on 9 February, soap was rationed in Britain aiding and abetting the cult of shabbiness, and 'Bomber' Harris assumed command of Bomber Command on 22 February.

News in March

In this month Singapore fell and the Japanese moved on to Java and Sumatra: Rangoon in Burma was evacuated. On 4 March Utility Clothing was introduced into this country: hemlines became shorter and it was the end for trouser turn-ups and double-breasted suits, yet another triumph for shabby.

On 6 March the petrol ration in Britain was halved and the *Daily Telegraph* was reduced from six to four pages on Saturdays but was spared the disgrace of being labelled 'unpatriotic' and 'critical of the war effort', the charge levelled at the *Daily Mirror* by Home Secretary Herbert Morrison on 19 March.

This comment may have had something to do with a Zac cartoon in the paper. On 6 March this depicted a torpedoed sailor adrift in the middle of the ocean and the caption (suggested by the controversial *Mirror* columnist, Cassandra) was 'The price of petrol has increased by one penny'.

There was uncertainty over what this meant: did it mean that some people were in far greater peril than the reader? Or did it mean someone was risking their life for profiteers at home? The government took the latter interpretation and carpeted the editor and Cassandra, who promptly departed for the army.

The clothes ration early in 1942 was enough to provide an overcoat every seven years, a pullover every five, jacket and trousers every two and underpants every two(!). You also needed twenty months for a shirt and eight months for a pair of shoes. 'Make do and mend' became popular although the working classes were not impressed since they had always done this.

The war continued. At the Imperial Hotel in New Delhi on 29 March, Alan Moorehead was ready to bet anyone 10 to 4 against India being invaded within three months, 10 to 5 against Turkey being invaded within three months and 10 to 7 against Australia being invaded within three months. He won all three bets in three months.

News in April

On 6 April it was the end for white bread in Britain: bread was now 'off-white'. Pam Ashford in Glasgow had got a new job with the Ministry of Fuel and Power. She wrote about the exhibition on 'British Arts Today' but noted rather sadly that the museum room specialising in stuffed birds had a notice on the door explaining that due to enemy action the birds were not looking as well as they used to.

About the same time, René Mouchotte's Free French squadron was protecting bombers over Caen. His compatriot, Béchoff, returned from the raid in a rather disgruntled frame of mind.

'A fine thing to be doing!' he complained bitterly. 'What a bloody war! I'm going to resign. I've had all I want. I'm packing up!'

'What's the matter, Béchoff,' scolded Mouchotte, 'did you take the seagulls for Mes? How many did you shoot down?'

'Oh, go to hell! I think it's pushing patriotic zeal a bit far to go and protect the bombers of a nation that goes over our country to bomb a power station I'm a stakeholder in.'

Elsewhere, English ladies of the genteel class were very enthusiastic about adopting a French pilot each. There were all sorts of offers – such as cars and the like. The City of Ottawa adopted a French squadron and sent over 25,000 fags for them.

April was a terrible month for the Allies in the Far East. on the 9th 76,000 American and Filipino troops surrendered and were then marched 65 miles in conditions of great privation and brutality – it was called the March of Death. Many perished on this dreadful trek, and many more after they arrived in the POW camp. At least General Wavell was holding out in Corregidor.

The 248th day of the siege of Leningrad was marked on 15 April, as was the resumption of tram transport in the city. During this month over 100,000 citizens died from enemy air raids, starvation and sickness.

Baedeker Raids on British cities commenced with Exeter and Bath on the night of 23/24 April. 'Baedeker' was the railway guidebook and the Luftwaffe's idea was to attack historic cities. Norwich and York (a shop in the city advertised 'Wreaths and Crosses. No Tomatoes') also suffered during this month but 70 per cent of the dwellings in Rostock were destroyed around the same time. Hitler was livid and Goebbels declared that 'The English belong to a class of human beings with whom you can talk only after you have knocked out their teeth'.

Some of these 'human beings' in Britain, mothers with young children, wanted to do part-time war work but there was a shortage of day nurseries. Protests by Hampstead mums led to headlines in the *Picture Post* magazine: 'Hampstead Mothers Stage baby Riot to Demand more day Nurseries'. Some young mothers were able to get work at home. Emily Golder of Finchley assembled small aeroplane parts. She collected the bits and brought them back home in a pram with her small son perched on top.

By now, music over loudspeakers at work was becoming very popular, especially the BBC programme *Music While You Work* (our favourite second line for this was 'Hitler's a dirty twerp'). Workers could perform their tasks to the tempo of the music. At a munitions factory in Acton the favourite was 'My old man said "follow the van"', rendered vociferously by all management and staff.

I was in a gang of boys touring the streets with a cart collecting anything spare for the war effort. Brownies in my area collected enough to fund a Spitfire. We also sung lustily – 'There'll always be a dustbin' to the tune of *There'll Always Be an England*. Meanwhile, residents in the borough sought scapegoats for all the war damage. In their eyes, Councillor M.H. Davies was to blame.

The Benedictine monks at Belmont Abbey feared that the nearby city of Hereford would be next on Goering's Baedeker list and formed their

'There'll always be a dustbin', 1941. (Reproduced by kind permission of the Trustees of the Imperial War Museum (HU36208))

own fire brigade, with a proper fire engine and splendid uniforms. In April my father, my mother, my sister and I moved to a three-bedroomed council house in Cubitt Town. It had been damaged by a land mine and repaired. It was now set in the middle of a desert-like terrain of large bombed-out areas, the result of a pasting by land mines which caused extensive lateral damage. After the war prefabs and orlets (two-storey prefabs) were assembled with the help of German POWs. The orlets are still there – going for about £200,000 these days.

News in May

On 14 May German torpedo bombers sank the cruiser *Trinidad* off Bear Island. It was escorting one of the convoys trying to get supplies through to Russia via Iceland and Archangel. Surgeon Lieutenant Maurice Brown swore that the torpedo which sank the cruiser had 'acoustic powers'.

'It followed the bloody ship around till it found it,' he explained to his rescuers. He knew more than he thought he did – they were 'acoustic torpedoes' which did follow ships about.

In Berlin an anti-Soviet exhibition was set on fire by well-wishers (in fact, anti-Nazis). The Japanese advanced deeply into Burma. Whilst dysentery was now almost as dangerous to Allied troops:

'Ah'm crappin' ivvery colour bar blue,' admitted an infantryman from Cumbria of the 9th Battalion of the Border Regiment.

The first thousand-bomber raid of the war was on Cologne on 30 May. 'An advance payment from Bomber Harris', the Jews of the city described it as. Lord Haw-Haw announced that the raid was a triumph for the Nazis on the basis that the hell that Bomber Harris was inflicting on Germany would be repaid with interest, so the more the merrier. Harris did not need encouraging.

News in June

In June Ernest Bevin, the Minister for Labour, could be found reflecting on a recent headline in a national newspaper: 'Bevin wants a hundred thousand women: the State to keep the children.'

The Battle of Midway Island early in the month was a disaster for Japan – four aircraft carriers and a cruiser sunk, 332 planes lost and 3,500 men – sweet revenge for Pearl Harbor and a critical turning point in the Pacific War. American radio made the most of the news in broadcasts to Germany by Professor Henry Hatfield of William College. His German had an American accent so listening Germans did not regard him as a traitor as we did Haw-Haw. In this month Haw-Haw said that children in Britain were being fed with bad fish from the USA. An evacuee, 'J.G.' of Suffolk, thinks this referred to Kennylands Camp School in Sonning Common in Berkshire because he could distinctly remember the baked cod served up one day.

John Houseman ran the broadcasting station The Voice of America for the Office of War Information. John was actually born in Romania and so 'the voice of America' was technically an alien.

Schools did have their problems in those days: austere Miss Score turned up at my school in one black and one brown shoe. She had a lot on her plate.

It was probably Lord Haw-Haw who spread the rumour that Nazis ate children for breakfast. Cynthia Gillett certainly believed in it and kept well clear of the German POW camp in St Neots. However, the Italians in their cage seemed very nice. 'Come-along-a-da-fence. We give you a big-a speak-a.'

Cynthia was having all sorts of experiences on evacuation. At Dartford Girls' Grammar School in Kent it was all 'notes up your knickers and that sort of thing'. But at the mixed Huntingdon Grammar School she found life far more sober – apart from the Italian POWs.

News in July

The magazine *Vogue* announced that grey hair was fashionable, saving much anguish over the lack of hair dye. Cosmetics in general were difficult to come by. But to smear lips with beetroot juice (quite effective, actually) was one in the eye for Hitler, who detested all make-up.

'Balszup' was how one merchant ship captain described the fate of Convoy PQ17 to Russia. Someone gave the order for the escort force and convoy to scatter because of 'superior enemy forces' in the vicinity. Nineteen out of thirty cargo ships were lost (100,000 tons, including 430 tanks). What Lieutenant Richard Walter of HMS *Ledbury*, one of the escorts, said about the mix-up was totally unprintable and libellous.

Someone was happy, at least. Hans Schmidt, to all intents and purposes a German spy, who was working on a farm in Dorset, managed to get a cryptic message through to his German masters: 'Will be out of touch for a fortnight. Just got married. Going on honeymoon.'

If he really was a genuine spy he was getting fully integrated into British society. The message, of course, may have been an attempt at a joke.

The Australians were fighting in New Guinea and compatriots were trying to keep up their spirits in Changi gaol in Singapore with a spot of frog racing. It was well organised: each contestant had a printed pedigree and a name. There was 'Easy Money' by 'Petrol' out of 'Nippa'. Each frog was also decorated with its own distinctive colours. They were placed in a box in the middle of a square. The first to reach any part of this perimeter (they went off in all directions) was declared the winner. In order to keep these thoroughbreds in top racing condition they were fed on white ants.

The prisoners had to work in the docks unloading supplies but the Japanese guards became irritated at the increasing rate of stolen goods. They were given a stern lecture about it by an irate guard commander. He placed a tin of condensed milk on the ground, put a cloth over it, demonstrating that his men knew all the little tricks of the prisoners. When he removed the cloth the tin was gone.

News in August

In August, the winner of the Red Cross Stakes at Wembley dog track ('Whirlwind') was seen later in the month at Workington Stadium racing as 'March Hare' and as an outsider. As part of the 'Dig for Victory' campaign, the swimming baths at the ladies' Carlton Club in Pall Mall were converted into pigsties.

Meanwhile, in our back yard on the Isle of Dogs, only 30ft square, we kept chickens and grew potatoes. I was reared on egg and chips – it's still my favourite meal. Elsewhere, George, my dad, had three allotments – one in the churchyard, one in the ex-park and one on the Mudchute. I had to weed all three of them.

American forces launched Operation Watchtower on 7 August, invading the island of Guadalcanal in the Solomon Islands, but the German army reached the Caucasus oilfields on the 9th. On 19 August Canadian and British, American and French troops raided Dieppe. Ominously, German Commander-in-Chief von Rundstedt had recently declared that 'Dieppe is a most unsuitable place for a landing'. It was riddled with a network of machine gun nests and anti-tank guns.

The French squadrons provided some of the air cover. This followed a visit from General de Gaulle. René Mouchotte was in charge of ceremony for the occasion. 'Pilots! Attention for the Commandment!' he ordered loudly and got the finest outburst of general mirth he'd ever generated. More successfully, Mouchotte was later awarded the

Croix de Guerre with Silver Star plus two Bronze Palms by the general, and the march past was led by a very fat WAAF whose posterior wobbled alarmingly.

At Dieppe the French soldiers wore their distinctive red pom-pom hats rather than tin helmets and the citizens of the town were overwhelmed to see them. They rushed to bring out food, drink and presents. One commando was presented with a large bag of eggs by a very enthusiastic madame and he continued the war with grenades in one hand and eggs in the other.

On a more serious note, another French commando paid a special visit to the Mayor of Dieppe and stuck a bayonet through him. It seems they had a history.

The raid was a disaster: three-fifths of the attackers were killed or captured. Also, when Ordinary Signalman Les Seldon's boat arrived back in Newhaven harbour the port refused to open the gates as it was past closing time. The authorities eventually relented. Les went home on leave the next day.

'I've been to Dieppe,' he told his mum.

'Oh, have you, son? That's nice.'

One survivor of Dieppe was Sooty the cat, who was from Newhaven. She elected to have a kip in a landing craft and thus unwittingly took part in the raid. She returned with a torn ear and stone deaf. She was the only female on the expedition and was awarded the cat VC and her picture was in all the papers.

Four days after Dieppe, on the River Don at Izbushensky, the Savoy cavalry from Italy (all 600 of them) armed with sabres and hand-grenades, charged 2,000 Russians who had mortars and machine guns. It was the last successful cavalry charge of the war (or ever, probably). The Russians ran for their lives. The Germans were almost in Stalingrad but the Japanese suffered another disaster off the Solomon Islands.

For Stalingrad, Hitler ordered the elimination of the entire male population, communists being regarded as even more dangerous than Jews. The entire female population was to be 'shipped off', where to or what for was not made clear.

At home, the British were now confronted with at least forty-eight official government posters advising them about how to live:

'Eat Wholemeal Bread', 'Do not waste Food', 'Keep your children in the Country', 'Find out where your nearest Rest Centre is,' 'How to Behave in an Air-raid Shelter', 'Look out in the Blackout', 'Carry your gas mask at all times', 'Join the Auxiliary Fire Service', 'Fall in with the fire-bomb Fighters', 'Report for Civil Defence Duties', 'Help Build an Aeroplane', 'Recruit for the Air Training Corps', 'Save for Victory', etc. ...

Ernest Bevin, however, did complain graphically about national wholemeal bread to the deputy prime minister during a Cabinet meeting. 'I say, Deputy Prime Minister, that this loaf is indigestible,' and proved his point with a loud belch. 'There are, you see,' he added, 'what did I tell you?'

News in September

On 13 September escaped British POWs were rescued from a beach near Perpignan by HMS *Tarana* in Operation Bluebottle. In the same week, Soviet marines, hiding in a giant grain elevator in Stalingrad, picked off the Wehrmacht in the streets below. Himmler arranged for the 'delivery' of 'asocials' – Jews, gypsies, homosexuals, Russians, Ukrainians, Poles who had been in prison for at least three years, and Czechs and Germans who had been inside for eight years or more.

Denholm Elliot, a RADA hopeful, reported to a bomber base on 23 September to be a wireless operator in one of the crews. He was greeted by the service engineer: 'Good luck, son, the last wireless operator on this kite got a cannon shell up his backside.' But at least Elliot would keep warm; wireless operators in Lancasters were usually roasted and rear gunners froze. He met the crew and they had the normal two pouches for their personal effects, one for the wife and one for the girlfriend. There was time for a few drags on a fag and a piddle up the tail wheel for luck.

News in October

On 7 October Dr Herbert Linden, the German Minister for the Interior, suggested to Hitler that the corpses of the people they murdered should be burnt in case they were dug up later in history and gave future historians the wrong impression of Nazism, but Major-General Odilo Globocnik, who had an important position at the death camps, disagreed. His idea was to put up bronze plates to indicate how brave the Nazis were to complete this gigantic and onerous task.

In the ruins of Stalingrad two enormous armies fought on in pouring rain, and bad weather also did for Leif Larsen, a Norwegian naval officer who tried to sink the *Tirpitz* with a couple of 'chariots' in a fjord on 26 October. These were manned torpedoes but he was undone in a sudden squall. Japanese sub-mariners had tried something similar in Sydney harbour on 31 May. They had midget submarines but missed the American cruiser *Chicago* and hit a converted ferryboat.

Late in the year

Billy Hill, king of the London underworld, pulled off perhaps the most daring of his robberies. His associate, Slippery Sam, was an agent for lorry-loads of 'surplus' parachute silk supplied by an RAF officer in East Anglia. But Billy and other associates, disguised as police, waylaid a large consignment in a Suffolk lane. It saved him having to pay for it.

On 5 November Operation Leonard aimed at depositing a large supply of Bren guns and other weapons on the Algerian coast as a prelude to Operation Torch. But the local resistance fighters had got mixed up with the dates and the British commandos were not impressed.

At 10 a.m. on 2 December Enrico Fermi, the Italian émigré nuclear scientist, gave the order for the first self-sustaining nuclear chain reaction in the rackets court at the University of Virginia. 'The Italians are extremely lax in their treatment of Jews', Goebbels wrote in his diary on 13 December.

As the year ended, the Axis Powers were in retreat in Libya, Guadalcanal, New Guinea and the Caucasus and were on the cusp of disaster outside Stalingrad. 'Oboe', a radio beam, directed British bombs on to targets in Düsseldorf on a cloudy night. The tide was also beginning to turn in the Far East – a limited offensive into Arakan (north-west Burma) from India. Sergeant Clifford Webb of the 1st Battalion of the Royal Welch Fusiliers noted that the Japanese soldiers often shouted over in English, 'Your wives are waiting for you'. The CO shouted orders in Welsh, totally bamboozling the Japanese.

Back home, in the WVS centre in Barrow-in-Furness on Christmas Day, one serious soul was concerned about the general air of hilarity amongst helpers and ack-ack personnel.

'Should we laugh at these boys?' worried this lady.

But a gunner leaned forward and leered at her, asking, 'Shall we have a kiss now or do you want something later on?'

Women got their own back at a sten gun factory in Peckham, South London. Only one worker on the shop floor was male – Charlie Draper, a rather innocent lad. His female colleagues sent him on various errands – for elbow grease, and long 'weights' for pregnant women. Eventually, however, they sought even more excitement and removed his trousers and underpants and sprayed his testicles with varnish. Charlie spent two hours in the toilet with a thinner.

In Berlin Lance Corporal Norman Norris, a POW, liked to sing with his fellow prisoners on their way to work. They particularly liked to render 'Hi-ho, hi-ho, and off to work we go' from *Snow White and the Seven Dwarfs*. In order to improve the visual impact of their performance they walked along on their knees banging their picks on the pavements. They made a lot of noise and there were numerous complaints from sober Berliners.

ELEVEN

Early 1943

The Far East

The year began with Japanese forces being overrun in Buna, Papua New Guinea. In Burma, Operation Cannibal sought to drive the Japanese from Chittagong towards Donbail but Allied prisoners on the Thai–Burma railway were enduring horrific conditions whilst being worked till they dropped.

Fun could be had: Don Maclean, an Aussie, and compatriots were building a 'pack of cards' bridge over a gully. They took every chance to try and drop something on their captors from on high. But the guards wanted fun, too. 'More sing, more sing,' they ordered, being fans of the Australian vocal efforts. '*Icky, nee, nisio, nisio*' ('one, two, pull, pull') they chanted as they dragged up huge steel girders.

Suddenly, a guard 'fell' from the higher reaches of the half-built bridge. But a hand shot out and caught the guard by his collar.

'Drop the bastard! Drop the bastard!' the prisoners yelled.

'I can't,' called back the 'saviour', 'I pushed the bastard but the other bastards saw me.'

John Lever, a ground crew member of 84 Squadron, RAF, was also a prisoner – on Moji Island, Japan. On 23 January he lay in the darkness, trying to sleep after another day's hard slog. Suddenly, he sat upright and called out to his fellow inmates, 'I could murder a treacle pudding!'

'Shut up, shut up!' they screamed back. It was worse than torture.

A few days later a friendly guard slipped them a swede. But it was as hard as iron. They tried to smash it against a wall and stamp on it. Some bits did fly off it and they pounced on these like hungry wolves. The result was the raving trots.

Bombing Germany

On 16 January 1943 British bombers attacked Berlin for the first time since November 1941. Following this, Churchill and Roosevelt issued a joint directive from Casablanca outlining a policy of bombing Germany day and night. With a casualty rate of 1 in 20, bomber crews on tours of thirty sorties rated their chances of surviving a tour were about 50:50. But, as Sergeant Protheroe at RAF Wickenby put it, 'I'm looking forward to saying "up yours" to old man chop'. As a reprisal for the Berlin raid London was attacked for the first time since May 1941.

Also at Wickenby, Flight Lieutenant Tony Smith suffered from nausea every time he got back from a sortie and so there was a ritual of preparing a full tankard of beer ready for him in the mess. He drank this straight down and at that moment fellow pilots and crew made them themselves rapidly scarce as noxious fumes escaped from Tony's nether regions accompanied by sounds like rolling thunder. Several minutes of this would see him back to normality.

It was Tony's plan that he and his crew should fly round and round in circles over the sea, submit forged navigator and bomb aimer's reports and pretend they had gone to Germany. He was only joking – but, apparently, one bomber had really tried to do this, although not from Wickenby.

The United States 8th Air Force made its first raid on Germany – Wilhelmshaven – on 27 January. This force actually shot down twenty-two German fighters over the port. However, on leave, these heroic crews appeared as less impressive in their pink trousers and drab olive jackets.

'Them trousers will be filthy before they know it. Their clothes don't even match,' remarked a Liverpool lass after her first encounter with American air crew.

On 30 January British bombers attacked Berlin during the day and Hamburg at night. The enemy air force responded and south-east England had its first experience of the 'cuckoo' air-raid warning – an addition to existing sirens. The 'cuckoo' meant, 'They're overhead, mate!'

It was the tenth anniversary of Nazi rule and Goebbels celebrated in a radio broadcast: 'A thousand years hence, every German will speak with awe of Stalingrad and remember that it was there that Germany put the seal on her victory.'

The next day the commander of the German Sixth Army, Von Paulus, was promoted to field marshal and he promptly surrendered to the Russians outside Stalingrad, having lost 160,000 men. Another 90,000 were marched into captivity to Siberia – tens of thousands did not survive the journey.

February

During this month the Japanese were being forced out of New Guinea and Guadalcanal by Australian and American forces. In the United States, exempt men rushed forward to enlist. Herman Kogan was a Chicago journalist but he volunteered for the marines. Towards the completion of basic training the authorities eased him into becoming a combat correspondent. But, uncomprehending, his trainer stared at the drafting instructions for Herman.

'Combat correspondent? What the f**k is that?'

'As I understand it, sir,' responded the newspaperman, ' you write about the men in your outfit.'

'Waddya gonna do – fight the f***ing war with a f***ing pencil?'

'No, sir. You shoot first and then take notes.'

In Germany, Rommel seemed to be the only star left in the German High Command: he defeated an Anglo-American army in the Battle of the Kasserine Pass on 20 February. The officer in command of the Lothian Regiment lost an arm and Sergeant Cadger lost the opposite arm and for years and years after the war they only bought one pair of gloves at a time and shared them.

'Cheesey' Flynn was also involved in this action. He was batman to the new second-in-command in Reg Crimp's battalion. But Cheesey was not a happy man because his captain had been in a very cushy job in Cairo.

'Quids in dahn there 'e was,' declaimed the servant to Reg peevishly. ''Uts to live in, spring beds to kip in, char and wads every morning. Casino every afternoon. Cor blimey! Could 'ave roughed it dahn there for the duration, mate, easy. An' so could the boss – could 'ave 'ad 'is pick of the cushy jobs, even worked 'is ticket back to Blighty. But, no – 'e 'ad to get back to the old shower. Wrote to the colonel 'speshly (I shuftied the coggage). Some blokes want their brains tested. But 'e's quite a good sort, really.'

'Shuftied' was one of those Egyptian words adopted by the Desert Rats (7th Armed Division). The only trouble was that Tunisian was a different language, which led to some confusion. For instance, the soldiers had the habit of saying, 'say – eeda', upon meeting Tunisians (it meant 'Go with God' in Egyptian). The Tunisians thought they were saying 'Good morning' (English and Egyptian being equally incomprehensible to them). Being a polite race, they repeated 'say – eeda' to the soldiers.

Capturing Tunis was taking far longer than expected. Alan Moorehead, the war correspondent, came across soldiers at this time who were quite bitter and hostile.

One private said to him, 'They said the last war was the war to end all wars. I reckon this war is supposed to start them all over again.'

Another Tommy was even more aggressive: perhaps it wasn't personal – he just did not like war correspondents in general: 'Are you the bastard what wrote in the papers that we're getting poached eggs for f***ing breakfast every f***ing morning?'

News was better in the Far East where Brigadier Orde Wingate's Operation Loincloth drove deep into Japanese-held territory in Burma. His outfit (the Chindits – 77th Indian Infantry Brigade, containing a medley of troops, including some stroppy Liverpool dockers) had mixed opinions about Wingate. Some thought he was a god, others thoroughly disliked him.

He was certainly a fearless daredevil who had nothing but contempt for the enemy. He drove his officers mad with his alarm clock and his

Flit (anti-malaria) Gun, which he carried and squirted everywhere. Some of his close associates were also rather eccentric, such as Major Michael Calvert with his boxer's flat nose and cauliflower ears. Colour Sergeant Harold Atkins of the 2nd Battalion of the Queen's Royal Regiment remembered Brigadier Bernard Fergusson wrapped in a towel still with monocle and a vast beard.

The first Chindit expedition resulted in the loss of nearly a third of the 3,000 strong force after difficulties in withdrawing from Burma, where they were trying to disrupt enemy communications and generally make a nuisance of themselves. Their exploits tended to be rather glamourised in order to impress the Americans, hoping for their air support in addition to the RAF. Wingate was promoted to general.

He was also hoping for some American soldiers, 'Merrill's Marauders', but in the event General Stilwell refused to lend them. 'You can tell General Stilwell he can stick his Americans up his arse,' was Wingate's spirited response to this news. Sadly, in the spring of 1944, during the second Chindit expedition, he was lost in a B-25 crash.

In New Guinea there were further views of officers. The Aussie well known as 'Whacker' was 'old' – getting on for 30 – and he had very definite views. He despised Pommy publicans, Egyptian 'gulli-gulli' men, Brummy coppers and Italian barbers. He also had little time for military policemen, 'poofters, pimps, Japs and poons', but, above all, officers.

His close mate, 'Johnnie' (Peter Pinney), tried to find examples of decent officers but Whacker was having none of it (quoted from Richard J. Aldrich's *The Faraway War*):

Johnno, I don't know where you growed up but it weren't nowhere where I've been. You don't know your arse from Pancake Day. I been a lot of places, boy, I done a lot of things. I've fought a lot of bastards, too: and one or two was better than me but not many. I've met ponces and drongos and dimwits and villains and pricks and plain damn fools, but the biggest menace in this man's world is some ninety-day wonder from the Reserve Officer Training Corps what pushes good men into

> action without knowing what he was about, and gets 'em killed. Wrap
> a pisspot in silk and what you've got is still a pisspot.

A round-the-clock air offensive was launched on Germany on 25 February, British bombers by night and American by day. 218 Squadron at Langan near Nottingham took part and Sergeant (later Flight Lieutenant) Wallace McIntosh, DFC and Bar, left a detailed description of his appearance at this time. Generally, he believed, he resembled 'a dead yellow whale'. He had an electrically heated suit over his RAF trousers and on top of that was a gunner's 'Taylor' flying suit with large buoyancy pockets over the knees, elbows and collar. They looked like built-in Mae Wests, designed to allow crew to float in the sea if they ditched.

McIntosh and his comrades could not get into this lot without each other's assistance: they dressed each other. He also wore a big white and warm jersey and his lucky grey, maroon and white scarf his granny had bought for him. At least he avoided the women's silk stockings which were favoured by some American airmen.

The zeal in collecting scrap metal at home was unabated. A proud local newspaper headline in Somerset proclaimed 'Smash in the Eye for Hitler. Burnham-on-Sea railways for Scrap'. Meanwhile, RAF police thoroughly scoured London for airmen who failed to salute officers. 'Britain Blanco's while Russia bleeds' read graffiti on a wall in Stepney.

March

McIntosh was in sorties against the Ruhr industrial heartland and Berlin which grew in intensity as well as frequency whilst a lone German raider over Scotland jettisoned a single bomb onto a wild and lonely moor and struck a store containing 70,000 gallons of whisky.

The cunning plan to blow up Adolf Hitler with a bomb disguised as a parcel of liqueur (Operation Flash) on 13 March failed because of a defective detonator. There were growing protests in the Fatherland against the Nazis. On 3 March a worker in the capital gave up his seat on a tram to an elderly Jewess.

'What do you think you are doing?' demanded a Nazi official.

The defiant worker looked the Nazi up and down and retorted, 'I'll do what I like with my arse, if you don't mind.'

Protests multiplied about the behaviour of American soldiers in Britain and a top-brass conference on moral laxity was convened in London. It heard that venereal disease was 50 per cent higher amongst American servicemen in this country compared to those at home in the United States. Apparently, one of the main reasons for this was the blackout. Fault could not be entirely laid at the feet of individual men: in one outfit the storeroom was 'heaving' with 30,000 condoms ('rubbers' to Americans). Commanders at the base pleaded with other ranks to do something about the problem. Conference lambasted GI moral depravity whilst the GIs moaned about too many Brussels sprouts (and queuing – although they got to quite like 'fish 'n' chips').

It could have been down to tight puttees: if the GI still had some circulation they were too loose and if you could button up a uniform it was not tight enough (if it stayed with you when you moved it wasn't loose enough).

Possibly, the centre of depravity was London's Piccadilly, where 'front-line commandos' called out, 'Hey, Yank, quick, Marble Arch style', an invitation to a 'wall job' or 'knee-trembler'. The girls believed that doing it standing up avoided pregnancy.

In 1943 Shepherds Market, which was between Piccadilly and Mayfair, compared favourably with the red light districts of Genoa or Marseilles. A local resident complained about the wrong sort of letter being shoved through her letterbox.

'The Rainbow Centre' in Shaftesbury Avenue was a place where GIs could get a meal and a drink, some dancing, a book, a writing room, bed and entertainment. Outside, on the pavement, there was a nightly gathering of market traders.

'Anything to sell?' they asked every soldier going in or out until the 'Snowdrops' (American Military Police) moved them on. The centre even had a 'prophylactic clinic' to minimise the chances of catching something nasty from the Piccadilly commandos. Snowdrops were everywhere because of the crowds of American servicemen in the city. They had to know the London streets better than taxi drivers, and were often seen giving directions to Londoners. 'You can't miss it,' they added, in parody of a favourite British phrase.

Further up the road the 'Hyde Park Rangers' worked a fourteen-hour day occasionally trying to up their prices to innocent-looking Yanks and getting the traditional response, 'Honey, I want to rent it not buy it'.

One Piccadilly stalwart was infiltrated into the Alert Room at the airbase in Seething and remained there at work for ten days. Suspicions, however, were aroused when it was realised that men presenting themselves for VD protection all came from the same hut. She was sent back to town.

Courts martial were held in Grosvenor Square under a large stars and stripes. On the judge advocate's desk was a revolver, and lanky marines at his side had side guns and batons. There was no oath and counsel questioned witnesses seated and with arms folded. A witness

'Got any gum, chum?'
(Photograph by
Richard Reynolds)

– a colonel – strolled in smoking a cigar, placed it in counsel's tray and gave the president of the court a perfunctory salute.

Back in the provinces blown-up rubbers tended to decorate jeeps and in Bedford some were floated down river past the startled gaze of upright citizens. Much younger citizens generally welcomed the Americans. 'Got any gum, chum?' they ritually chanted (the reply was often 'Got a sister, mister?' This actually meant 'Have you got a jam jar?' due to the shortage of glasses in pubs).

One particular GI had no gum so handed over a 12in cigar to some kids and they were off sick from school for several days.

At Christmas Santa Claus appeared near bomber bases all over the country, one of them in a Flying Fortress. Clark Gable at 351st Bomber group at Polebrook and James Stewart at Tibetham were regarded as 'regular guys'.

Thousands of GIs married English girls. They had to be determined because there were fifteen documents to get signed off. One proposed in Barbara's Bun Shop in Bedford and at the reception a bottle of vodka was poured into the orange juice and animated some elderly relations.

'Triumph in Tunis' ran a headline of 28 March. The enemy 'Mareth Line' defending the city collapsed, even the 21st Panzer Division, feared by the Desert Rats. 'El Alamein was a picnic compared to the 21st,' reckoned Reg Crimp's signaller pal.

'You was in Cairo during El Alamein,' Reg pointed out.

'Well – I heard about it,' said the signaller lamely.

RAF Wickenby

On 27 March the RAF dropped twice the tonnage of bombs on Berlin as the Luftwaffe did on London on 18 April 1941, the heaviest raid of the Blitz. Crews were desperate for entertainment in the few hours between sorties. Canadians at Sutton-in-the-Forest in Yorkshire got the village pub's pet Alsatian drunk. Australians on Wellingtons at Wickenby near Derby seemed to have less fun because a favourite chant of theirs was:

This bloody town's a bloody cuss,
No bloody pubs, no bloody bus. Nobody cared for bloody us,
Oh, bloody, bloody, bloody!

However, when RAF Wickenby finally got inebriated anything was possible. Warrant Officer Ronnie Ainsworth from Guernsey tended to run about, often into WAAF shower huts. Wickenby had songs of rejoicing:

Old King Cole was a merry old soul, and a merry old soul was he.
He called for his kites in the middle of the night, and he called for his rear gunner three.
Every rear gunner was a fine type, and a very fine type was he:
'Jesus Christ, it's cold,' said the rear gunner.
'Corkscrew port like hell,' said the mid upper.
'Dah-di-di-dah di-di-dah,' said the wireless op.
'We are bang on trail,' said the navigator.
'Left, left, steady – dummy run,' said the bomb aimer.
'I want four pounds boost,' said the engineer.
'I don't give a f**k,' said the pilot, 'merry, merry men are we,
There's none so rare as can compare with the boys of Wickenby'.

Other actual conversations en route for Germany were more unrehearsed: 'Mid-upper to skipper – permission to leave the turret.'
'What for?'
'I want to leave the turret for a few minutes.'
'Yes – I said "What for?"'
'Well, er – I think I've shit myself, skipper.'
'What do you mean you think? Are you ill?'
'No, I've just shit myself. I thought I was farting but I wasn't.'
The skipper refused permission because night fighters were in the area. Other crewmembers continued the discourse. 'Too many baked beans, George.'
'Too much beer, more likely.'
'Let it bake, mid-upper.'
Coming back, over the North Sea, the skipper remembered George's little problem. 'Okay to leave the turret now but make it snappy.'

'No, it's okay, skipper, it's gone hard.'

There were more party tricks back in the Wickenby messes. The game 'Are you there, Moriarty?' had blindfolded protagonists trying to bludgeon each other with rolled-up newspapers whilst a choir sang at the piano. Then the front door burst open, in roared the station commander astride a powerful motorbike and completed circuits of the mess, trying to improve on his time every tour round. The men playing bridge in the centre of the room hardly noticed. George Gerrard staggered up to the medical officer, shaking horribly all over, his head jerking madly about and his face twitching uncontrollably.

'Tell me I'm fit to fly, Doc,' he grunted. 'I was pretty bad this morning but I'm okay now.'

'Yes – you look alright to me,' agreed the medic.

'Gee, thanks, Doc,' said Gerrard in a hoarse whisper and lurched off to the toilet retching whilst the choir sang on to the tune of the German National Anthem:

Home presents a dismal picture, dark and dreary as the tomb;
Father has an anal stricture, mother has a prolapsed womb.
Sister Mary has aborted for the forty-second time.
Brother Tom has been deported for a homosexual crime.
Little Willie's in the mad-house, Doctor says he's in for good
And the cause of his affliction ...

The wing commander had also been eating glass as his party piece since 1927. The M.O. had issued him with plenty of warnings. 'The build-up of arsenic will get you.'

'Balls,' said the wing commander, and ate some more.

Meanwhile, the trick of the deputy gunnery leader, 'Jumbo', was to burst into someone's room, pretending to be drunk and brandishing a revolver, which he loosed off through a window and then turned on the 'victim'. The gunnery officer himself had been the 'victim' so many times that he'd had enough and so one night he produced his own gun and squeezed the trigger. Jumbo slung himself face first on the lino and subsequently desisted from his bad habits, except that of breaking wind violently at dinner.

At home in April

There was good news and bad news. 'Holy Smoke!' penned Pam Ashford in Glasgow, 'the points rationing scheme is to cover breakfast cereals now.' There had been rumours about this dreadful turn of events and Pam had hoarded ten boxes of Weetabix, two of Ryvita and one of Corn Flakes.

Lord Woolton, Minister of Food, seemed to be an honest bloke being up-front about frequent cock-ups in food supply and rationing. 'I know the troubles you are having,' he said in a radio broadcast during April. 'It's a frightful mess but we are clearing it up and it won't happen again.'

On 20 April Mr Churchill announced that the ringing of church bells could be resumed. Since 1940 this had been the agreed signal of a German invasion.

Jean Stafford, from Ladywell in South London, had been evacuated to Bradford (her dad was stationed in the RAF there. My wife's family moved to Exeter for the same reason and her father was promptly sent to North Africa). Jean recorded that the kids in Bradford knew all the names of the Allied generals and she called her cat 'Timoshenko'. I had a cat called 'Scraps'.

There was much tension over people believed to be shirking enlistment to the armed forces, especially conscientious objectors or 'conchies'. One man, who wrote an anonymous diary, recounted that he was an irreplaceable expert in making certain engine parts from scrap metal. He was continually insulted and his father-in-law was always trying to explain the situation (he couldn't reveal what the engine parts were involved because they were top secret).

'Ah, f**k off willya. We all know exactly what that c*** is,' was a typical response, this from a 12-year-old girl.

The sight of women doing what was formerly men's work still did not seem right to many. For instance, some bus passengers believed that female bus clippies had sex with the driver before clocking off every night. However, pressure was exerted on both sexes to volunteer for fire-watching duties, despite the protracted absence of the Luftwaffe. It was remarked that only a congenital idiot could fail to avoid fire duty and congenital idiots were exempt, anyway.

Upper-middle-class residents living in the West End of London were officially asked what they could offer in the way of public war service. One lady offered to drive a car on any day except Thursday when she went to visit her husband in Kent. Another offered herself and her maid from 5 p.m. to 7 p.m. except at weekends when they went to the country.

TWELVE

April-August 1943

North Africa

In April, the Axis forces were being driven into a small pocket of territory around Tunis. Montgomery spoke to an American general at the beginning of April.

'What would you give me if I took Sfax by April 14th, eh?'

It was a highly unlikely outcome so the general answered, 'Anything.'

'What about a Flying Fortress?'

'Yeah,' (since it was so unlikely).

Sfax fell on the 10th and Monty sent a signal to General Eisenhower. 'Fortress, please.' Ike suggested that he should wait till the campaign for Tunisia was over but Monty insisted on his B-17 right away. The ensuing dialogue was brusque with the result that the B-17 was delivered along with a crew to fly it. They were very happy; flying around with a general was an easy ticket.

Reg Crimp's battalion was not so happy. By now it expected to be sent back to Blighty. There were mumblings of discontent and the old soldier Sergeant Brandisham was livid at their attitude. 'I'll bleedin' well smarten up some of yuh bastards,' he screamed.

But the mutterings continued. Brandisham had completed his six years of overseas service. 'It's alright for him, the snide – he's on the next boat home,' was a typical comment.

But before he got on it Bandisham was killed leading his men to take an enemy machine gun post. Generally, however, morale remained high, buoyed by good news from the Eastern Front. A song was composed and rendered to the tune of the *Lincolnshire Poacher*.

That Hitler can't be beat is a load of cock.
For Marshal Timoshenko's boys are pissing through von Brock.

In both Libya and Tunisia the RAF dropped little wooden toys on the Afrika Corps. These consisted of a small figure of Haile Selassie who was buggering a small figure of Mussolini if a string was pulled. The German soldiers loved it.

At sea (and ashore)

At sea the revised U-boat Enigma key had been broken at Bletchley Park. An attack on a convoy in mid-April resulted in only one merchant ship being lost against the loss of U-175 by depth charger. Six other submarines followed 175 to the bottom and on 24 April they withdrew from the North Atlantic. But Lieutenant Bill Johnson was still worried about acoustic torpedoes which could track a ship's screws. Yet he survived this latest attack and had a double celebration because he was promoted to the post of secretary to Captain Walker.

Captain Walker himself was on form and performed his usual party trick of standing on his head and drinking a glass of beer. When he invited someone else (not familiar with the captain's brand of humour) he poured the beer down the trouser leg of the unfortunate victim.

Bill Johnson was bedevilled by enemy technology because there were also 'Chase-me-Charlie' guided missiles on gliders released from German bombers. However, to Bill's relief, it was soon discovered that electric razors messed up the homing systems on the gliders and turned them round on their parent planes. All you had to do was have a shave ...

215 Squadron raided Stettin and Rostock late in April. The Lancasters flew low at 200ft to keep below the radar, and over the Baltic Wallace McIntosh's plane sucked up the icy spray and soaked the bomb-aimer, Sammy Craig, crouching in the well below the pilot.

'Fred,' he complained, 'can we go up a bit, I'm soaking wet.'

'You're lucky your electric suit is switched off,' Fred the pilot reminded him, 'otherwise you'd be fried meat.'

On 30 April a body purporting to be 'Captain Martin' was washed up on a Spanish shore. He had with him secret official documents indicating that the Allies would soon land in Greece, rather than Sicily. This was Operation Mincemeat and it was a hoax the Germans fell for, apart from Goebbels, who guessed it was an elaborate piece of deception but was averse to telling Hitler so.

The body, in fact, was that of a Welsh vagrant called Glyndwr Michael obtained by Flight Lieutenant Charles Cholmondeley, who, according to Churchill, had the right sort of 'corkscrew' mind to outwit all except Goebbels. Cholmondeley, he of the great height and wax moustache and with an intense interest in the mating habits of insects, put together a convincing packet of personal effects to persuade the Nazis that 'Martin' was genuine. He even used voluminous underpants which had belonged to the Oxford historian H.A.L. Fisher. German High Command moved men and armaments from Sicily to Greece.

David Smiley of the Special Operation Executive was ashore with Albanian guerrilla forces, a red star in his hat and giving Communist salutes to all and sundry.

'Very infra dig for an officer of his Majesty's Royal Horse Guards,' he mused to himself.

Tunis in May

Tunis was captured on 7 May and the city witnessed scenes of wild confusion: Allied troops mixed with Germans and Italians in crowds which thronged the narrow streets whilst enemy snipers still lurked in dark corners. French citizens threw flowers over them all.

The 'prisoners' were still walking out with their girlfriends and taking a shave at the barbers. The logistics of rounding them all up was a nightmare. They didn't care; for them, the war was over.

Ted Smith, of the Army Catering Corps (ACC), had his own problems – with Italian-built toilets, a task they were very good at. They were so expertly disguised that Ted kept falling down them. And they were very deep – and smelly.

Ted buried thousands of tins in the desert – meat and veg, bully beef, cheese, milk, jam, potatoes, peas, pilchards, baked beans, soya, bacon, sausage, biscuits, flour, sugar, tea, rice and porridge – it all came from tins. And Ted was only one of many cooks who also buried hundreds of tins. The Western Desert has millions of interred tins.

It was possible to obtain anything in Tunis – one just took it. Alan Moorehead searched for transport. 'Take your pick, mate,' an officer informed him and Moorehead selected a Fiat. The only difficulty was that it was crammed with Italian officers, but they were quickly sent on their way. Moorehead drove it up the road and the engine blew up.

His next choice was a Volkswagen and this proved to be reliable: the journalists drove it 600 miles to Algiers.

Ted Smith never ceased to marvel at the Arabs. The Army Catering Corps were generally regarded as the top-notch thieves of the whole Eighth Army but the Arabs easily out-pinched them due to a lack of discrimination. They stole anything, even off Ted, who himself was the champion felon of the whole ACC.

A German officer gratefully accepted tea and biscuits from Ted, who bore no ill feelings towards the enemy. It was 3.30 in the afternoon, time for tea. The prisoner presented Lieutenant James Wilson with his field glasses in recognition of the kindness and Wilson used them to watch the cricket at Lords and Trent Bridge in 1946 and thereafter.

On the Tunis tip Ted encountered an American machine-gun crew whom the war had somehow forgotten about. They were quite happy camping out in the desert because they had thousands of tins and plenty of water. They spent their days playing poker and they owed each other millions of francs. They said to Ted that the only thing that would move them would be when the tins or the water ran out.

He left them to it but he had a sneaking admiration for them since they were men after his own heart.

The Desert Rats (7th Armoured Division) now had a well-earned rest and enjoyed lizard racing (they tried crabs but they insisted on going sideways). Civilians who had wisely evacuated Tunis now returned, including Madame Phillips, a Russian dancer who had settled down with a Frenchman. She was with a party of singers and transvestites. She recalled the electric train stopping so that young German soldiers could relieve themselves out of the windows. A priest took the opportunity to alight and go along telling them about God so they urinated over him.

Out on the Tunis tip La Baronne lived on in a sumptuous palace overlooking the sea but she bitterly complained to Ted Smith that the dreadful Italian troops had roasted her pheasants on barbecues set up on her front lawn.

'C'est la guerre,' said Ted.

The RAF in May

On 13 May 1,000 tons of bombs were deposited on Bochum in the Ruhr in forty-five minutes. Operation Pointblank was about to begin aiming at the destruction of the German economy, its military system and the morale of its people. Wallace McIntosh (207 Squadron in Spilsby) was promoted to flight lieutenant and celebrated with a night out in Skegness. He encountered some ladies who presented him with a knitted koala bear adorned with medals and a parachute. On his return to base comrades told him that every crew which had been given one of these bears were gonners. Wallace carried on to survive two tours – fifty-five sorties.

Pilot Officer Fotheringay-Jones had brought with him rave reviews of his Spitfire training unit but on arrival (in a Spitfire) at his posting he performed some dangerous manoeuvres. Squadron Leader Watson tried to discipline him but Fotheringay-Jones told him to 'Go and get stuffed'. The station commander also tried his luck but was told to 'Go and have a good shit'.

'That will be all, Watson,' the commander said to the squadron leader, 'for myself I am just going to the lavatory. I have no doubt you will make your own arrangements.' Fotheringay-Jones was the nephew of the Secretary of State for Air.

The 'Dambusters' also had their own arrangements (16 May). So did Winston Churchill, flying back to England from Tunis. He took over the controls at one point and escorting fighters had great difficulty in trying to elude him.

Elsewhere in May

Peace terms were offered to Hitler in an advertising campaign: 'A new type of Government for Germany and back to fresh butter, cream cheese and Crawford's Cream Crackers.'

Rationing hit ladies' knickers. They now came under Utility Clothing regulations and were limited now to only six styles.

Some population movement was caused by the need to re-site industries vital for the war effort, such as the Telecommunication Research Establishment to Malvern in Worcestershire. Evacuation difficulties ensued because many potential hosts were reluctant to share their accommodation and suddenly discovered elderly aunts who were coming to live with them. Even those who accepted the situation created strict rules for the lodgers, such as being in by 10 p.m. or not coming in till 10 p.m.

Meanwhile, queues still proved irresistible to citizens even if they only walked away with a bunch of roses and a stick of rhubarb.

Out in the Far East the idea of a 'mating season' at Changi gaol in Singapore was a popular idea amongst married internees being kept apart, but there were serious objections from older and more substantial wives. One such lady was scathing about the plan: 'What,' she scoffed, 'give the Black and Tans a chance to breed more brats.' Malcolm, a New Zealander, wrote home to his loved ones from a prison camp in Japan:

I trust you don't mind the number of squashed ants on these pages. The topmost ant on page two was not of a large size but with long, thin legs which enable it to get along at a terrific speed. I call these the 'greyhound ants'. They can cross page two in two seconds while other ants of large size take seven seconds to do it.

Allied troops in North Africa were awaiting the signal to invade Sicily. In the Kerrata Gorge area, Mahmoud, who was a frequent visitor to 56th Heavy Regiment, Royal Artillery, in his quest for extra fags, offered to lead a party of gunners to the haunt of some wild pigs in the mountains. Leaving at 7 p.m. they followed Mahmoud for an hour and then he advised them to hide in a tree in order to detect wandering pigs. By midnight he had smoked every fag they possessed and there was still no sign of any pigs. All was quiet – not even a grunt – when Mahmoud delivered a terrifying fart.

'Christ!' gasped Sergeant Dawson. 'No wonder the Crusaders lost.'

At home again, the latest government poster creation was the 'Squanderbug', a leering, hairy creature awash with swastikas,

Queue for horsemeat, 1943. (Reproduced by kind permission of Mirror Syndication Ltd)

inciting housewives to waste money. *It's That Man Again* (*ITMA*) on the radio continued to entertain hugely: Tommy Handley was now 'His Washout the Mayor of Foaming-in-the-Mouth' and prided himself on the motto 'Loosen the green belt, tuck in the blue points and paint the town red'. More amazing characters featured, such as 'Ali Op', the pedlar ('I go, I come back') and the 'Diver' ('I'm going down now, sir' – a catchphrase copied by many bomber pilots), 'Hari-Kari, the Jap' and 'Signor So-So' ('A Mistair Handpump, I am diluted to meet you').

In fact, you could listen to good wireless programmes all day, pausing only to cook dinner (during the news in Norwegian) and dish-up supper (during the news in Gaelic). *The Brains Trust* was very popular with learned men discussing questions sent in by the public, such as 'Why can't you tickle yourself?' (which actually stumped the experts).

Clothing restrictions continued to bite hard. Humphrey Lyttleton's Uncle Richard, a steel executive, decided to go to work without socks, exhibiting naked flesh under his pinstripes whilst in the City.

There was a continuous search for unrationed food. The restaurants in London's Granada cinemas offered 'Roast Eagle and Veg'. Lord Woolton, Minister of Food, popularly known as 'Uncle Fred', continued to advise the country on healthy eating in his frequent broadcasts. During May he condemned all those 'superior' people who turn up their noses at fish and chips – 'tasty, sweet, first-class grub' he called it. The lord was formerly Fred Maquire, a social worker from Liverpool.

A national debate on absenteeism from work rolled on, with the political Right condemning it and the Left blaming the Right for it. It was almost impossible to sack anyone because of the difficulty of finding someone to replace him or her. Employees, aware of this situation, could become very cheeky with superiors. For instance, a bus driver told an inspector, 'Drive the bloody bus yourself' after being caught having a crafty cuppa at a mobile canteen en route. The inspector did 'drive the bloody bus'.

June

Anglo-American agreements poured forth all the time as Churchill and Roosevelt showed close co-operation. However, Max Beaverbrook noted on 17 June that the British prime minister regarded the American president as a repetitive bore annoyingly prone to getting out his stamp collection during conferences.

Beaverbrook also recorded that Churchill reckoned that Madame Chang-Kai-Shek was a lesbian because there was a young woman permanently in her entourage without any discernible (political) role.

The 56th Heavy Regiment, Royal Artillery, was in Ziama Bay when on 22 June 'a wild Sirocco' gale blew crowds of monkeys into their camp and they ate all the NAAFI buns. 'They'll all be dead in a week,' reckoned Driver Kidgell.

A bulletin from the government during this month announced that illegitimate births had grown by 65 per cent since before the war. Police continued to be vigilant because of rising crime and a diligent constable apprehended Pilot Officer Currie near the Wickenby bomber base riding his bike without lights (in the city it was an offence to ride one with lights). The efficient copper recorded the incident in fine detail, including Currie's remarks.

'You'd do bloody well in the Gestapo. I hope your f***ing rabbits die.' They had obviously met before.

The day and night bombing of the Ruhr increased in intensity. American losses were very heavy. John Steinbeck remembered crews winding each other up by asking for shoe, collar, waist and length measurements. 'What size shoes you wear, Brown? I get them if you conk out.'

They had also to endure more Brussels sprouts and warm beer. Henry Crain, a junior radio officer, suggested to his gunner that they should have another beer in the pub. 'What for?' demanded the gunner. 'This stuff hasn't even got enough character for you to dislike it.'

Operation Bellicose consisted of 'shuttle bombing'. For instance, on 20 June, after a raid on Friedrichshafen, the bombers flew on to Algiers. On the way home, they attacked the Italian naval base at La Spezia.

Not surprisingly, bombers occasionally got lost. Pilot Officer Currie landed at a strange airbase and pulled up by the watchtower. 'What airfield is this?' he called out.

'Eh?' came the elegant reply.

'Where are we?'

'What do you want to know that for?'

'Because we're bloody lost.'

'Oh. Can I see your identity card?'

'Get stuffed,' suggested Currie. 'Who do you think we are – the flaming Luftwaffe?'

July and August

At Chequers early in July Noel Coward played 'Don't let's be beastly to the Germans' for Mr Churchill and four nights later the Allies landed in Sicily. By 22 July General Patton had captured Palermo. In August local girls watched soldiers swimming in the nude in a cove outside Syracuse. Mussolini was under arrest and Hamburg was a smoking ruin after five continuous days of bombing.

As the conquest of Sicily progressed the Grand Fleet held sway in adjacent waters. HMS *Illustrious* sent up its new 240mph Fulmers so that other ships could recognise them. As they toured around they shot down two Italian bombers just for the fun of it. Landing back on *Illustrious* they were whisked into the interior of the ship by electric lift. The whole operation had taken about ten minutes.

A sailor watching this performance on HMS *Warspite* walked over to the creaking hangar on the deck, which housed two ancient 100mph Swordfish and scratched on the door, 'This way to the Museum'.

In Sicily Flight Lieutenant Tom Hughes became the only RAF pilot to bail out of an enemy plane. At Comiso they found some serviceable Messerschmitt BF 109s. Hughes took one up only for the engine to conk out and he had to parachute out.

Later, he was shot down in his Spitfire over Monte Cassino, badly burning his legs. He was imprisoned in a hospital. There, he told a

German general that the Spitfire was better than the Messerschmitt. For this indiscretion he was put into solitary confinement, which, he believed, saved him from being used in drug experiments by German doctors.

U-boats in the Atlantic were also on the receiving end of advanced technology – Enigma de-coding, air and sea searches, homing depth charges and aerial torpedoes. Seven submarines were sunk in thirty-six hours on 13–14 July.

The Russians were advancing and so were the Americans in the Pacific. 'The whole Fascist movement went pop like a soap bubble,' General Jodl said to Hitler. The raid on Hamburg on 28 July caused a firestorm and an internal hurricane.

While all this was going on Private 'Big Train' Mulligan was making the American army work on his behalf. He drove a colonel around London for a job. On 4 August there was a big party on a ship anchored in the Pool of London. Big Train made straight for the fridge and made a pile of very thick beef sandwiches containing enough ration meat for several families over several weeks. He was interrupted

Fun at Stalag Luft VI, Heidekrug, August 1943. (Dolby)

by the colonel, who had become fed up with the party since there was not enough booze going round.

'Right, Mulligan, it's time we got along.'

'Yes, sir. I thought the Colonel might be a bit hungry. There are these beef sandwiches.'

Big Train was learning the local lingo fast and he was producing a sort of Georgia-cum-Oxford-cum-Camden Town dialect. He went around saying 'Cheer up, mait.' But he still refused to believe that he could not get petrol in a gas station, although he did consent to referring to lifts and braces.

As the colonel stuffed himself with beef sandwiches nearby kids on the dockside were on the lookout for gum or candy, or anything remotely edible. They became interested in a crate of rubbish – in fact, squeezed orange skins. They seized handfuls of these and squeezed out the remnants of the juice observed by an understanding copper.

'Very 'ungry for horanges they are,' he explained to passing pedestrians. 'I 'aven't 'ad an horange for four years. It's the law, ain' 't? No one hover 5 years old can legally 'ave an horange.'

In Virginia, a 'Sewer Pipe Atomic Test Bomb' was dropped on a naval proving ground on 13 August. On 18 August two German 'spies', 'Jack' and 'OK', otherwise known as 'Mutt' and 'Jeff', depending which side you were on, pretended to blow up an electricity generating station in Bury St Edmunds. It was even reported in *The Times* and called Operation Bunbury.

The Battle of Berlin began on 23 August as 700 British bombers were sent across. Pilot Officer Currie survived and his crew celebrated by reviewing the administration of the swear box. The going rate was one penny for a four-letter word, twopence for obscene gestures, threepence for 'subtle verbal variations' and fourpence for 'downright blasphemy'.

A heated row ensued in the mess about who had said what, only producing even more bad language. Finally, the majority of the crew indicated they were ('bleedin'-well') backing out of the scheme due to the paltry charge of sixpence charged on one crew member for uttering a sentence in which he used every vile word known to man plus unheard of combinations of them.

THIRTEEN

September–December 1943

September

On 3 September General Montgomery invaded mainland Italy – with an army. The Italian authorities had made no arrangements for this contingency.

On 8 September Donald Wheal's mum told him the war was over.

'What – over?' he enquired.

'Only Italy, though,' his mum explained.

Also on the 3rd, 346 Berliners were killed in air raids. The next day Lord Haw-Haw broadcast from Hamburg. 'Now that we have survived into the fifth year of the war I will only say that German victory is certain'.

Thousands of Italian soldiers were murdered in Rome by their former allies. On 12 September Mussolini was rescued by a squadron of German gliders from the top of a mountain and whisked to Hitler's HQ in Rastenburg.

In Kinsayok camp on the Thailand–Burma railway, the Japanese tried to solve a case of cholera by shooting from a distance at a tent housing the patient.

Harold Wakefield, who flew a Halifax in 51 Squadron, enjoyed the raids over Germany – at least, that's what he wrote in a letter to his parents. He thought the lights in Hanover looked very pretty, just like the Blackpool Illuminations. He also thought that eggs and bacon before taking off and on return made the whole business worthwhile.

October

Naples fell to the Allies and the war artist Edward Ardizzone was in the city on the first of this month. He was accommodated in a rather seedy hotel, which had a brothel on the first floor. A kind concierge came round with a blowtorch to exterminate the bed bugs. Ardizzone went shopping in Pompeii and purchased a (rubber) phallus as a present for the officers' mess. Kids were begging for 'Caramela, caramela' (candy) from American troops.

The Australians were making good progress in New Guinea, just like the Russians on their own soil, but the Nazis had murdered a million Russian Jews. Himmler held a conference of SS leaders to celebrate. 'Most of you know what it means to see a hundred corpses lying together, five hundred, or even a thousand. To have stuck it out and at the same time, apart from exceptions caused by human weakness, to have remained decent fellows ...'

Noel Coward was performing in Cairo on 6 October. Afterwards, he wanted a swim but had no swimming trunks so he borrowed an enormous pair of underpants belonging to Lord Moyne.

'Where's the lav to put 'em on?' he enquired of a gathered audience. 'I need a shit, anyway.' He emerged wrapped in these colossal pants and was introduced to a lady. 'Simply amazing,' he told her, taking her hand, 'definitely no sign of shit paper.'

The next day Pilot Officer Currie was once again forced to land at a strange airfield when his engines failed. They sent back a carrier pigeon to base. 'Only carrots to eat here – send help'. The pigeon flopped down on a nearby hangar roof and refused to budge.

'Get homing, you idle bird,' shouted Currie. 'Steer three-six-o.'

'Chuck a stone at it,' suggested a gunner.

'No – I think it's tour expired,' said Currie.

'Nah – you can't expire on an abort.'

On the same day, Schmidt, the German 'spy' in Devon, signalled once more to his German masters. 'Am proud father of a seven-pound boy'.

The Allies were on their way to Rome. Edward Ardizzone was in Ravello and threw a party in his usual extravagant fashion but it was gatecrashed by locals. 'The men,' he recorded in his diary, 'were the most frightful shits but the girls were okay.'

On 13 October Italy declared war on Germany and joined in the campaign to capture Rome. On the 15th a small Anglo-American commando unit landed south of the city in enemy territory in order to rescue an Italian admiral and his wife. The project was delayed an hour because they didn't know the commandos were coming and the lady hadn't packed. She proceeded to fill up a trunk so large that the commando leader had to make a separate return journey to collect it.

Ardizzone was in Compobasso, where the weather was freezing. He was lucky enough to be with the 'Army Fowl and Pig Unit' (renowned for being able to sniff out a pig several miles away) and so he ate pork and chicken for a few splendid days.

John Steinbeck recalled a 'Pig' with wonderful and mystical powers. It was a lucky wooden charm for bomber crews. Pig was all-knowing.

'Pig, this one is not for us. Pig, you know the one that gets us, gets you.'

Pig could also produce a fog out of a clear night, smooth down a rough sea and even procure a steak in a restaurant which hadn't seen one for weeks. This particular Pig had been around for generations and had been responsible for the commutation of executions and cures for all sorts of illnesses and at least one big win on the horses.

Other American servicemen preferred a different source of solace: Fred C. Robbins, a soldier in India, favoured a local liquor labelled 'Assam delivery', but re-named 'After Death' by the Americans.

Churchill was flying back from Italy on 19 October when a steward threw an admiral's teeth into the chemical toilet. He, the steward not the admiral, had no alternative but to plunge his hand into the icy, blue depths of the Elsan, and all ended well when the admiral popped them back, unaware of their recent travels.

November

On 5 November the Russians re-captured Kiev, their third largest city. The news from the Far East was also good as Captain Mike Lowry with the Queen's Royal Regiment pressed on with General Slim's 14th Army towards Imphal and Kohima.

'We are right behind you, sir,' he said to the general.

'Don't believe it, boy,' he replied, 'I am about 200 miles behind you.'

Lieutenant Bill Johnson was aboard HMS *Starling* hunting U-boats in the Atlantic. Evidence of 'kills' had to be substantiated by hard evidence. Short of something more solid the ship's doctor pickled some human remains and sent them by parcel post to the Admiralty, where they were opened by a WREN on 6 November.

Frank Keegan was having his own sort of problems in the American Navy. Ordered to attend a 'short arm inspection' he admitted to a pal that he thought his left arm was, indeed, shorter than his right one.

On 14 November, in a daylight raid on Germany, escorting fighters shot down twenty enemy fighters. Down below, in the POW camp in Moosburg, a dentist extracted one of G.C. Bateman's teeth – unfortunately, the wrong one. But he did have an anaesthetic, unlike Italian and Yugoslavian prisoners. Bateman's guard kindly wrapped a scarf around his face.

'Tomorrow we get the right one,' he assured Bateman.

'Thanks a lot,' replied Bateman.

Hundreds of Berliners were now being killed every day. On 22 November 'Papa' sat in his old wicker chair and refused to budge during the raids so his family loyally stayed with him rather than go to the shelter. A bomb fell in the street and the family jumped up in fright but Papa didn't move a muscle.

'Sit down,' he ordered. 'That way, if the ceiling collapses you will be further away from it.'

Even Hitler's personal train, the Amerika, was damaged. Goebbels had no heat, light nor water supply in his house. Prototypes of new army greatcoats were also destroyed – a great pity because the plan was to show off one of the coats to the Führer and put a bomb in one of the pockets.

Lieutenant Dennis Rendell, who had been captured in Tunisia, escaped from a POW camp in Sulmona in Italy in September and formed a resistance group made up of other escaped prisoners, plus some Italian Partisans. He was even in touch with the British ambassador in the Vatican City.

He came down from the mountains when bad weather set in and took up residence back in the town of Sulmona. One day in November Rendell and six other escapees visited a travelling fair and mixed with German soldiers and airmen. Two Luftwaffe were trying their luck at a rifle range but they were so bad that Rendell grabbed the weapon and hit the bullseye with his first shot. This hit triggered a photograph of Rendell and the Luftwaffe. Rendell's comrades were getting a bit nervous by this time and grabbed the film and made a rapid getaway.

Later in Rome Rendell went up to senior German officers at the opera hoping they would autograph his programme. His German was non-existent and he could barely speak Italian. He came back to his mates proudly displaying his trophy.

'You know who that was, Dennis, do you?' asked a comrade.

'No.'

'That was the Military Governor of Rome.'

Rendell rose to the rank of brigadier and became provost marshal of the Royal Military Police. He died in 2010.

December

On 9 December Lieutenant D.P. James of the Royal Navy also escaped from a POW camp but continued to wear his standard naval uniform because there were so many uniforms in Germany at that time he hoped nobody would notice. His ID card introduced him as a member of the Bulgarian navy called 'I. Bagerov'. Later, he turned into a Swedish sailor and reached Stockholm.

In Italy the German line at Cassino was under fierce Allied onslaught. Lieutenant Warren 'Bing' Evans of the 1st Ranger Battalion was ordered to take an enemy position with a frontal assault. This was not going to be easy so Bing called out to the foe across a gully:

'Anyone over there who can speak English?' he yelled.

'Yes,' replied an official voice. 'Do you want to parley?'

'Sure do,' responded Bing. 'Let's stand up together, shall we? I'm Bing. What's your name?'

'Hans.'

They stood and Bing set out his terms. 'You give up now and we'll introduce you to some nice Red Cross girls and a steak dinner.'

Hans had a good laugh. In the next few hours they had many conversations. He told Bing that his parents ran a hotel in Leipzig. Eventually, Bing had no alternative but to attack. Hans was killed. When Leipzig was taken in 1945 Bing stayed in a hotel and the current owners told him that an elderly couple had formerly run the place. Bing was convinced they were Hans' mother and father so he got their address and visited them.

They were, indeed, Hans' parents. On greeting them, Bing just broke down in tears.

In Naples Edward Ardizzone, the war artist, was complaining about the lack of decent restaurants. One he went to on 7 December was terrible and to add to his misery a dreadful tenor sang in his face. Alex Bowlby was having more fun in Regello. A crowd of local girls laughed at the pipe permanently stuck in his mouth.

'Pipone!' they called out. 'Pipone! Pipone!'

Bowlby chased after them and caught up with the slowest lass and arranged to meet her the next day. She invited him home and the whole extended family gathered to give him the once-over. Mama noticed that his fly buttons were missing and insisted on replacing them immediately. Off came the trousers and Alex sat there under the combined gaze of three or four generations.

In a summer residence of a cardinal, Bowlby came across a beautiful coat – embroidered in crimson and cloth of gold. He took a cap of the same material and two corks with silver tops (for the Holy wine). When he got back to England his mum made a lampshade out of the cap.

Not long after his visit to the palace he went down with dysentery and was sent to hospital. Whilst he was there a German shell struck the cookhouse.

'All the cooks was mixed up with the meat and veg,' a reliable witness informed Alex. 'All they found of Nobby was 'is 'and. They knew it was Nobby's because 'e bit 'is nails something awful.'

Back at Cassino Alex Bowlby was entertained by the antics of the Partisans – always good for a laugh. On one occasion they were preparing to assault a formidable German position just round a bend in the mountainside. They were armed with swords, which they flourished around their heads with gusto and intent.

'Avanti!' shouted their brave leader and round the bend they flew before a Spandau opened up and they came flying back round the bend and disappeared rapidly into a field of maize.

Local drinkers could be equally amusing. It being near Christmas the NAAFI gave a free issue of Guinness. But the troops should have known there was no such thing as a free Guinness: the gift was sour. Alex bartered it for local wine.

The locals were ecstatic over the deal and as they consumed the rotten stout they became even more excited. 'Buono! Multo-buono,' they cried.

In Naples on 18 December Ardizzone was in a rented flat suffering with a hangover. To give him an even worse headache the landlord arrived – 'an objectionable and whining elderly Jew, bogus like his furniture' – with an equally horrible daughter. The reason for this unscheduled visit was the presentation of an extraordinary and absurd inventory for the flat suggesting that everything in it was of enormous value.

This was bad enough but the landlord also started poking about in other rooms and discovered the girlfriend dressing in the bedroom. Ardizzone had the devil of a job persuading the Jew that she was not a sub-tenant.

In Assam the Japanese were fighting back fiercely and the M.O. of Mike Lowry's battalion was forced to wrestle with one of them on 20 December. He knocked out the bloke's gold teeth and claimed them as a spoil of war. On Christmas Day no enemy patrols came out and indeed they played *Home, Sweet Home* on their gramophone – more fiendish torture. But they resumed firing on Boxing Day and drowned out the efforts of an ENSA accordionist and comedian.

Clyde Berwick, an Australian army engineer, had a better Christmas even though he was a POW, because he was taken off the gruelling work of building the Thai–Burma railway. He received a letter from his mum dated 1 August 1942 which got him up to speed on family fortunes. He celebrated by trying to make a Christmas cake but it was so bad that they fried it.

The last day of 1943 was a portent of events to come. Commandos were making frequent sorties to the Normandy beaches. On 31 December Major Scott Bowden and Sergeant Ogden Smith were crouching on what was to become 'Gold' Beach. Jerry sentries were only a few yards away. A few seconds before midnight Smith whispered into Bowden's ear.

'What?' replied Bowden.

'Happy New Year,' repeated the sergeant.

'Happy New Year,' responded Bowden.

At Cassino the Americans failed to break down the German defences. The Battle for Rome was going to be long and hard.

FOURTEEN

January-May 1944

The New Year

In January it was rumoured that Berlin's anti-aircraft guns were manned by 15-year-olds from the Hitler Youth and loaded by Russian prisoners. 'Clueless Kate', Pilot Officer Currie's Lancaster, survived but twenty-eight other bombers did not, so much for kids and Russians. 'Clueless Kate' was actually a junior intelligence officer at Currie's base, who, according to another rumour, liked to eat fish and chips as she indulged in sex.

On 2 January the headline of the *Sunday Express* was 'Russians 27 Miles from Poland'. Guy Sayer, a Frenchman in the German army, complained that whilst he ate soap civil servants administering the retreat to Poland had sardines, bacon, schnapps, cognac, wine and cigars. They also had their girlfriends with them – and 'spicy wurst' – and gingerbreads. 'Bastards!' wrote Sayer.

The Americans were also advancing in New Guinea and, apparently, successfully on Australian women while in Australia, much to the annoyance of Australian men. However, American and Australian soldiers under the command of General MacArthur got on quite well, much better, apparently, than MacArthur did with Admiral Nimitz of the American Navy.

Freddie Mathieson, an Australian army driver, had been delivering bombs to an American airfield at Manbulloo near Darwin for a year. Yet, on 17 January, he was rudely accosted by a pimply faced American sentry, who leapt out from behind a bush.

'What's the password?' he screamed out, sticking his gun in Freddie's face. Freddie told him where to shove it.

'What's the password?' the guard insisted in a high-pitched voice.

'What password? I've been delivering bombs for a year with no f***ing password.'

'What's the password?'

Freddie had had it. 'Tell your boss if he wants his f***ing bombs he can come and get them,' he informed the guard emphatically and signalled to all the lorries behind him to turn round and follow him back from whence they came. The upshot was that the pimply faced youth was sent back to the cookhouse from whence he came and the new lieutenant who had ordered the password (known only to him and the guard) was also sent out of harm's way.

The air attack on Berlin on 20 January was remarkable for the fact that one Lancaster crew missed the target by 30 miles but scored a direct hit on a depot and workshop quite by chance.

Meanwhile, children in Hamburg, much like the chimps in London Zoo, could imitate the air-raid siren to perfection.

The landing at Anzio behind the German front line in Italy took place on 22 January. Private James Stewart was congratulated by a naval telegraphist for being a brave soldier.

'Jack, mate,' responded Stewart, 'let me tell you something. I can't get off this tin box ship of yours quick enough. I'm scared stiff of the sea.'

'Gentle' Johnny Ramensky, the Glasgow safe-blower, was in Rome with the commandos breaking into enemy safes. As a reward for his services to the country his considerable crime slate was wiped clean. He also paid a visit to the safe in Goering's Luftwaffe HQ.

Assam – Kohima

Captain Lowry, in Wingate's Army in Assam, chronicled the struggle for Kohima in great detail. By February 1944 rations were short and even 'Vec' fags were smoked in desperation: they were made from low-grade dung. Tensions were high as they were boxed in on four sides by Japanese counter-attacks and the new CO objected to the use of Hindustani in the officers' mess, even *chai* (tea) and *chota peg* (whisky), which officers used almost without thinking.

'I won't have any hurgery-burgery spoken in my mess,' he declaimed sternly.

Another view of the precarious position Lowry's battalion was in was to regard it as an 'impregnable box'. The terrain made such an interpretation possible because it was impossible to see the enemy in the dense jungle and impossible for the enemy to see them. In fact, on 5 February, the Japanese, anxious to get out of the torrential rain, slept in the 'Ascot Car Park', the battalion's transport lines. They had tried to put the Japanese off this course by putting up notices such as 'Tottenham Court Road – Highly Dangerous' and 'Charabancs use this road at their own risk'. But the Japanese were smart: they crept in after dark and crept out again before dawn.

On 5 February a message from the supreme commander, Lord Louis Mountbatten, was received by the battalion: 'Hold on at all costs. Large reinforcements are on their way', which was rather strange because Lowry and his fellow officers regarded themselves as on the offensive. Such confidence was justified when, on 6 February, all enemy positions were overrun and those kipping in the lorries were also apprehended. In one of them, a Japanese lieutenant was found to be in possession of six highly obscene postcards.

Food was now getting very short and a wild pig was hotly pursued to try and spice up a monotonous diet of dehydrated spuds. The call went out for a sharp dagger and Lowry lent his lethal Wazir weapon (and never saw it again). American Dakotas dropped some supplies.

'Sir, 'ere come our reinforcements,' suggested Private Travers. 'They're f***ing dehydrated Yanks.'

February wore on with the constant risk of being re-surrounded. 'Seen the news, mates,' announced Private Wells. 'Churchill says he's watching our front with interest.'

'Well, what I suggest is 'e ain't watching our f***ing rear,' said Travers. Despite their situation a concert party turned up to entertain. They had a sketch about two colonels whose logo was an elephant with the caption: 'The higher the formation the bigger the balls'.

The see-saw campaign continued for months but the Japanese attack on Kohima came in May. On 11 May 2nd Lieutenant 'Tiny' Taylor was wounded. This immensely tall warrior (a sad mess on the drill square) wore a broad grin, a cardigan, a watch and unlaced boots.

'Goodbye, sahib,' he said valiantly to Captain Lowry, saluted and tripped over his laces.

The monsoons were on but the rum ration had arrived. The CO led a frontal assault near Kohima on 12 May and fell headlong into an enemy latrine. But the battle was won by the next day and Captain Lowry lifted a corn-beef sandwich to his lips accompanied by a thousand bluebottles.

Joyce Grenfell

Joyce Grenfell started to tour with ENSA (Entertainments National Service Association) early in 1944. The first tour was to Algiers in January. She was welcomed by a lieutenant with acne, false teeth and no observable personality. The welfare officer looked like a brothel-keeper and had hit-or-miss rouge lipstick and a crumpled black dress.

On 30 January Joyce entertained wounded men in the hospital.

'Joe didn't do his Popeye impersonation last time we had ENSA,' revealed a patient. 'He does it ever so good. Go on, Joe.'

Joe was flat on his back with a leg strapped to a frame. He called for a sailor's cap, put it on sideways, removed his teeth and squashed up his face for a perfect Popeye. Joyce led the applause. Back in her digs at the Villa Desjoyeux the Dutch-Cockney cook presented her with a damp rose. It was made from a turnip.

On 3 February Joyce did three one-hour concerts in an afternoon. She got the nurses involved. Sister Barr, with a face 'like a friendly balloon', and Sister Pollard had been torpedoed in the Mediterranean. They recalled holding hands under the water.

'Oh, it does feel funny when a depth-charge goes off and you're floating nearby,' recounted Sister Barr. Another nurse sang *Just a Song at Twilight* and *I'll Walk Beside You* whilst performing a blood transfusion. She was warmly received.

January–April

Berlin was struck by 1,887 tons of bombs on 29 January. As a reprisal, the Luftwaffe dropped 37 tons on London (the 'Baby Blitz'). But there was no Allied progress in the battle for Cassino and thus Rome. The Germans were using a powerful rocket gun ('Mekelwerfer') – five rockets in a circle detonated by electricity. They made a high screaming noise so the Americans called them the 'Andrews Sisters'.

Hitler was forced to sack his cook in February after he discovered that she had a Jewish grandmother. The Baby Blitz resumed in March and Wilton's Oyster Bar and Spinks Club in St James's were damaged and the street was littered with medals and shellfish (according to Joyce Grenfell). In Sheffield on 9 March a lady rushing for shelter lost her pink knickers as the elastic broke.

The Japanese launched a massive counter-attack in the Solomon Islands and lost 5,000 men (the Americans suffered 300 casualties). The Japanese dead included a sailor, Kiyoshi Takeda, who had already noted in his diary that the war had sent him into a 'spiritual void'.

In 'Death Valley' in Burma Eric Murrell made Yorkshire Pudding because he was from Barnsley and he was fed up with corned beef. But his mates added jam to it and complimented him on his 'pancake'.

The Second Support Group continued to hunt U-boats in the Atlantic and Captain Walker was 'tickled pink' when he hit U-231 with a multi-barrelled mortar-bomb thrower. According to David Wheal's father in Chelsea, he acquired the U-boat commander's soft leather black boots.

The Wheal family was bombed out at this time owing to the Baby Blitz, the big one having missed them completely. The brick public shelters built in streets had become very popular. We used the one in Parsonage Street, Isle of Dogs frequently, but the perennial problem was whether the Fire Guard had opened it in time. He kept it securely locked owing to its popularity with courting couples and small boys taken short.

Don Peacock was a British POW on the island of Haraku. Each one of the thousand or so prisoners was presented with a small square of patterned blue cloth on the occasion of the emperor's birthday

(29 April). They would have preferred a decent meal. No one was able to ascertain what the cloth was supposed to be used for. Anyway, Don put himself on the waiting list for the one needle in the camp. He planned to make a pair of shorts.

He scrounged a bootlace to hold them up. A few days later they were ready and Don came on parade with his new pride and joy to loud acclaim, even from the guards. There was a large blue flower over his crotch and one covering his backside.

May

In May, Joyce Grenfell and Noel Coward were still entertaining the troops. Tony Benn watched Coward on 4 May singing a song about a grandpa who ate a large apple and made a very rude noise in the Methodist Chapel. Tony Benn remembered him using words like 'bloody, bitch, Christ, bastard, short arm inspection and sexy', despite the presence of ladies.

The successes at Bletchley Park (and other similar establishments around the world) in deciphering the vast majority of German Enigma messages is a famous story, but the ability of German intelligence to listen in to some conversations between Roosevelt and Churchill is less well known. Since Operation Overlord (the Second Front) was imminent this could have proved fatal to the project. But all that the listeners could ascertain was something was afoot.

The president signed off on 5 May with 'Well, we will do our best – now I'll go fishing.'

Perhaps the Allies would invade Norway? On 9 May the Swedish Stock Exchange was manipulated by British agents to push up Norwegian stocks by 20 per cent. A few days later a German 'spy' informed the German High Command that the First United States Army Group was in Yorkshire, which was a good place to kick off an invasion of Norway. The First United States Army Group did not exist.

On 16 May Thomas Price Lewis complained about the eighth boil on his bottom in Changi gaol, Singapore. On the 17th he received a bread roll for the first time since being imprisoned three and a half years before. On the 18th a Sikh sentry complained to the guards about being called 'a black bastard' and prisoners exposing their private parts in his presence.

The news was good from the Italian front, however. Monte Cassino was captured on 18 May and the Allies broke out of the bridgehead at Anzio after four months of frustration and joined in the advance to Rome. Major Fred Majdalany captured some sumptuous German magazines which destroyed the myth that Rhine maidens all wore dark blue stockings.

Private John Gordon got a cable from home – 'Son born both doing well love May'. Private Gordon had been away from home for two years and so he was understandably distraught and sought advice from Brigadier Clark, a good listener.

'Perhaps the message has been delayed,' he suggested kindly.

'Yes, sir,' said Gordon dutifully but entirely unconvinced. The next day he received a full letter from May Gordon.

Dear John,
Your Mum has a seven-pound boy. She's going to call him James.
Fancy having a step-brother,
Love, May.

But it was still very unexpected news. Mrs Gordon was a widow. Presumably, John had a stepfather now, too.

Thomas Mackwood, a 67-year-old accountant from Dulwich, fell asleep on a train on his way home and woke up in Hastings, which, in view of current activity in the South East, was an 'exclusion zone'. In addition, he had no identity card because his wife had thrown it away when she left him. He was sentenced to a month in prison and so missed all the excitement.

FIFTEEN

D-Day

Deception

During the first half of 1944 the Germans thought that the Second Front would be in Norway or Sweden or Pas de Calais or Normandy or Brittany or Bordeaux or Gibraltar or Marseilles or North Italy or Albania or Greece or Corfu or Romania or Turkey ... They mined the Bay of Biscay, just in case.

Rommel asked for the mining of the Bay of the Seine but was turned down. He also told Hitler that one of his Panzer divisions had no tanks. Operation Chattanooga, or Choo-choo, from 21 May aimed at the systematic destruction of railways in northern Europe and it was clear from decrypts that Hitler was firmly of the opinion that the Second Front (likely in Normandy or Brittany) would not be the main landing. This 'Third Front' would probably be in the Pas de Calais.

He also calculated that the main assault would not happen for several months from the start of June. In any case, his meteorologists told him the weather in June would not allow any landings, so Rommel left his HQ in La Roche Guyan in France and travelled to Berlin to have a chat with the boss. Meanwhile, German decrypters intercepted a message from the BBC to the French Resistance to cut all railway lines in northern France. They informed the people at La Roche Guyan but Rommel had left so they took no further notice of the information.

During the night of 5 June 3,000 ships were crossing the Channel, but German reconnaissance, hampered by the bad weather, reported nothing unusual. However, enemy radar did pick up on an enormous convoy heading for the Pas de Calais. This was, in fact, millions of metallic strips which had been dropped by the RAF.

Dummy parachutists were also dropped on Boulogne and other places, and German reserve forces rushed hither and thither. Motor launches and more electronic devices indicated activity towards Le Havre and Dieppe and Harfleur.

Hollywood was conspicuous in deception. There was a group of about 11,000 actors (including Douglas Fairbanks Junior), make-up artists, sound experts, painters, photographers and press agents who formed the United States 23rd HQ Special Troops (otherwise known as the Ghost Army). They continued to be useful after the landings: the illustration here shows bemused French citizens watching four soldiers lifting a 'tank' from one side of the road to the other.

An inflatable 'tank' being carried – a Ghost Army product.

Preparation

In preparation, there were also substantial innovations: 'Mulberry harbours' (artificial harbours), 'Phoenix' concrete boxes, 'Bombards' (brickworks), 'Gooseberries' (blockships which could be sunk to the seabed), 'Whales' (piers anchored to the sea bed) and, of course, 'Pluto' (pipe line under the ocean).

Trooper Peter Davies, 1st battalion of the East Riding Yeomanry, worked on making tanks watertight for landings off the coast. In the week before D-Day he was fitting additional armour plating. On the eve of his 21st birthday he stayed up very late, became very drunk and fell asleep on the job the next day. His friends kindly crept up on him and welded the steel heels of his boots to the tank.

Stirring from his deep slumbers Peter found himself unable to move and imagined that some sudden and dreadful paralysis had struck him down. But he soon understood his predicament and managed to squirm out of his boots. He then hacked them off the tank with a hammer and chisel. When he got back to camp they all sang 'Happy Birthday' and presented him with a nice cake.

Others were driving all sorts of novel tanks, trying to get used to them. Sergeant Kenneth Lakeman swerved violently to avoid a Canadian lorry and became one of countless servicemen who ran through the hedges of old ladies' gardens whilst they were gardening. This one said: 'You're the second tank that's dropped in this week. Have a cup of tea.'

Secrecy

Secrecy about the Second Front played a crucial part in preparation. On 31 May a London woman took her elderly mother down to Westminster Pier for a boat rip along the river to Greenwich. But there wasn't a boat in sight.

'There won't be no boats this month, love,' she was informed by a cheerful boatmen (happy to be paid for doing nothing except telling customers there were no trips). 'They've all gone to France for the Second Front.'

The construction of the Mulberry harbours was overseen by Brigadier Arthur Walter. A few days before D-Day he lunched well in a Piccadilly hotel with a colleague. On departing, well-oiled, he left his bag with details of Operation Overlord in it on his chair.

Rushing back he was greeted in the foyer by the hall porter. 'I have your bag, sir,' he announced calmly. 'I have it safe here in the lobby.'

A senior civilian employee at Eisenhower's HQ sent details of Operation Overlord to a post office in Chicago in a badly-wrapped parcel, having mixed it up with a present for his Auntie Mary. She returned Overlord to SHAEF in improved wrapping.

On 2 May the clue for 17-across in the *Daily Telegraph* crossword was 'One for the US' and already filled in as 'Utah'. On 23 May the answer to 13-down was 'Omaha'. Between 27 and 30 May the words 'Mulberry', 'Overlord' and 'Neptune' were also used.

The crossword compiler, Leonard Dawe, a physics teacher from Leatherhead, was visited by MI5, who discovered that he and a fellow compiler, Melville Jones, had spent a number of evenings with American and Canadian officers at a nearby bar. Dawe had no idea what the words meant.

On 3 June a teletype operator at the Press Association in Fleet Street was doing dummy runs in preparation for the Second Front. He typed 'URGENT PRESS ASSOCIATION NYK NEWS FLASH EISENHOWER HQ ANNOUNCES ALLIED LANDINGS IN FRANCE', then became distracted and actually sent this message to New York.

Within seconds other teletypers were sending 'BUST THAT FLASH BUST THAT FLASH EISENHOWER', but it was too late and crowds at sports stadiums in the city observed a minute's silence to pray for success.

In Exeter a railway employee found an entire set of Overlord plans in a briefcase left on a train. A dozen copies of Overlord orders were gusted out of an open War Office window into the street below. Frantic civil servants recovered eleven of them. But the twelfth copy remained lost for two hours when it was delivered to the War Office front desk by an upright citizen.

Escape

As the great day approached soldiers all over southern England were incarcerated under the guard of the Military Police. On 1 June men of the 3rd British Infantry Division were cooped up in Upton Park Stadium, normally the home of West Ham United. But that evening there came disaster: the NAAFI ran out of beer. Desperate infantrymen escaped to the Boleyn pub round the corner, mingling with the boozy elements of the local denizens for several hours of happy drinking.

Near Ipswich, Trooper Eric Smith (5th Royal Tank Regiment) also escaped into town with his mates. They went out on foot but after many happy hours they decided to borrow some bikes outside the pub to get back to camp. The CSM took parade the following morning.

'There was a bit of trouble in Ipswich last night,' he confided in them. 'Some of you characters disobeyed an order and went into Ipswich last night and the police are coming soon to identify you. This is the time for them who took part to leave the parade before they arrive.'

Senior officers tried to keep their troops entertained by other means. Bob Hope was over from the States with his brand of humour: 'You know what a barrack is – it's a crap game with bunks.'

Training

The Desert Rats (7th Armoured Division) were in training in East Anglia. They had got back from Italy in January. The 'tanned knees' had become a law unto themselves, dressing in gaudy silk scarves, brilliantly coloured pullovers and a range of exotic headgear (in deference to the local climate they did replace their shorts with trousers and sadly began to lose the tan on their knees). One tank commander sported a black silk top hat.

Other officers wore scuffed suede shoes and bright corduroy trousers, cultivating luxuriant moustaches. Needless to say, from top to bottom they had scant respect for authority, especially when

Military Police and Americans tried to exercise it. After a parade past Buckingham Palace the 5th Royal Tank Regiment became known as 'The Shitting Fifth'.

Bill Bellamy re-joined the 8th Battalion of the King's Royal Irish Hussars in Norfolk after a spell away with dysentery. He was allocated the same driver he had had in Benghazi. This was Bob Weir, M.M., who saluted respectfully and promised to look after Bellamy.

'A little f**ker like you needs protecting,' Weir added.

Despite all this tomfoolery the Desert Rats remained a formidable fighting force and breezed through exercises during a cold East Anglian winter and spring, christening them 'Shudder', 'Shiver' and 'Charpoy'. They learnt from new *Combat Rules* to shout 'Hurrah!' as it was designed to paralyse the nerve of the enemy, but the Desert Rats improvised with their own word.

Elsewhere, Sergeant James Bellows, 1st Battalion of the Royal Hampshires, was learning how to waterproof a watch whilst still being able to tell the time under water. The trick was to wrap it in a condom, squeeze the air out and tie a knot.

Troops received detailed briefings right up to the last moment. Americans were issued with a leaflet telling them about the French. 'Don't be surprised if a Frenchman steps up to you and kisses you.

D-Day. The guide to France appears amusing. (Reproduced by kind permission of the Trustees of the Imperial War Museum (B5207))

That does not mean he's queer. It means he's emotional. He's French and darned glad to see you.'

Sergeant Edwin Sinclair, an instructor with the 12th Field Training Regiment, Royal Artillery, brought in a general to give a last-minute pep talk. It was a striking example of leadership oratory, a heroic call to arms.

'The war's a f**ker,' he cried out with great feeling. 'Everybody thinks it's a f**ker. Monty's a f**ker but Monty's the f**ker who can fight the f**ker.'

By 4 June the invaders were moving towards the coasts. Alan Moorehead was amongst countless journalists reporting. He noted how units greeted other units.

'Blimey, 'ere's the f***ing Arsenal.'

'Careful, me dearies, don't overdo it.'

'Jesus Christ, what museum did they find you in?'

'When the f***ing frogs see you lot they'll give up.'

The paras arrive

Men of the 6th Airborne Division landed by glider at Bénouville near Caen just before midnight on 5 June. By dawn 18,000 paratroopers had arrived in Normandy, capturing vital bridges and disrupting enemy defences. Corporal C.D. Weighton, 12th Para, had shaken hands with the pilot on take-off.

'I haven't dropped paras before,' he said, and Weighton wondered whether this was a wind-up. Jokes passed between the paras waiting tensely in their seats, a fragile veneer of humour. 'Did you hear that Winnie wears a truss,' was one effort (it may have been true).

The landing at Pegasus Bridge on the canal into Caen came as a total surprise to enemy guards trying to get some sleep whilst on duty. One patrol was awakened in their neat little bunks by Lieutenant Fox. Eventually, they realised he was British.

'F**k off,' invited one of them, trying to get back to sleep.

Sergeant William Higgs landed safely in his glider and encountered a native hurrying along with a long loaf under his arm. 'Anglais,' greeted Higgs. 'Bonjour.'

The farmer shrugged and carried on rounding up a herd of cows. He couldn't give a toss for the Second Front.

Captain Guy Radman, a Brigade Signals Officer of 5th Para, conferred with his intelligence officer.

'Do you know where we are?'

'I've no idea,' admitted the intelligence officer, and they stared at a signpost which emerged out of the morning mist.

'Let's cheat,' suggested the captain, and the intelligence officer climbed on his shoulders and shone a torch at the signpost, obligingly left by the defenders and providing a detailed indication of where everything was.

Armada

A veritable armada of ships, including the missing Thames pleasure steamers, conveyed the invasion force across the Channel. As on the planes and gliders there were a few nerves. Private Andrews of the Royal Corps of Signals became very restless. He wandered around and casually opened the lid of a packing case. Inside it was a pile of white wooden crosses.

'Jesus Christ!' he cried out in anguish. 'They could have bleedin' well locked them up, couldn't they?'

'Cheer up, mate,' advised Sergeant Kenneth Lakeman, trying to maintain his men's resolve.

'Yeah, Andy,' added Private Fred Miniker, 'rest assured one of 'em's got your name on it.' The sergeant had to separate them.

Lieutenant Eric Ashcroft (1st Battalion of the South Lancashire Regiment) joined those at the rail being unwell into vomit bags. The enemy weather forecasters had done a good job: it was a rough sea. A man behind him called out desperately: 'Don't throw that one over! It's got my teeth in it!'

The parson of 147 Field Regiment, Essex Yeomanry, was trying to hold Holy Communion but the gale blew away his wafers. 'Bloody hell! Lucky fish,' he said philosophically and soldiers helped to chop up some bread with their jack-knives.

Ordinary Seaman Ronald Martin of HMS *Warspite* watched as they took on board a Russian admiral, a Russian general (Joe Stalin wanted proof that the Second Front was really happening), war correspondents and a very fat Chinese naval officer.

Martin and his matelot chums were complaining about the lack of any decent food. They did have 'action rations' – a large paper bag containing a 'tiddy oggy' (Cornish pasty), two apples and a bar of chocolate. The captain agreed to try a pasty.

'I must say this is most wholesome,' he commented and spat out the tiddy oggy into a vomit bag.

Ordinary Seaman Jack 'Buster' Brown was on board the minesweeper HMS *Kellett*. The vessel struggled back to England with a gaping hole in its side and a huge list to port. It ran aground and HMS *Arethusa* passed by taking the king across to France. It signalled to HMS *Kellett*.

'Well done'.

HMS *Kellett* replied: 'They're round and they bounce'.

Landing

The DD (Duplex Drive – or Donald Duck) Swimming Tanks with their canvas coats had mixed fortunes in the choppy waters at the landing beaches. Even when they floated well they were likely to be swamped or run over by DUKWs.

'Being a bloody sailor in a bloody tank is taking patriotism too far,' Lieutenant Stuart Hills of the Nottingham Sherwood Rangers Yeomanry complained. But the Germans had no idea they would use tanks at the outset of an invasion and would have agreed with Hills.

At 6.30 a.m. on 6 June Americans came ashore in their amphibious tanks at 'Utah' beach, at the western end of the invasion area, which, in total, stretched for about 50 miles. At 7.25 a.m. the British were on 'Gold' and 'Sword' beaches – Gold near Bayeux and Sword in front of Caen. Almost simultaneously, Canadians and British troops came ashore on 'Juno', between Gold and Sword.

Private Tom Bowles, 18th US Infantry, lost his helmet on Utah when a shell exploded next to him. Luckily, a few minutes later, he found another helmet and donned it.

'Where'd the hell you get that!' exclaimed his wiring buddy, John Lamm.

Tom took the helmet off and studied it closely. Inscribed on it was an eagle and the name 'Taylor'. It belonged to Colonel Taylor of the 16th Infantry Regiment but Private Bowles regarded it as a trophy of war and shoved it back on his head. After all, he needed a helmet.

On another beach, Lieutenant Elliott Johnson arrived in France on his back. He was just about to come up on the beach in his '155 Tank' (no turret, just a howitzer on top) and he signalled to the driver, Corporal Rackley, to accelerate. But Rackley mistook the gesture and braked violently, sending his commander somersaulting onto the wet sand, to loud acclaim from a gun crew sitting around

Corporal Bob Roberts, Canadian army, captures the tallest soldier in the German army during the Battle of Normandy. (*Bournemouth News* Picture Service)

smoking fags and reading comics. Also nearby was a colonel sitting in his staff car reeking of whisky.

'Welcome to France,' he slurred.

The only stiff enemy resistance to the Americans was on 'Omaha' beach, between Gold and Utah. They only advanced inland 1 mile by the end of the day. Elsewhere, progress was several miles deep.

By midnight 155,000 Allied troops were ashore but the German High Command still did not believe this was the real invasion, as was read from encrypted messages. This had much to do with the efforts of 'Garbo' (Juan Puyol Garda), a double agent sending misinformation to Berlin via Madrid. His message had been clear – the Normandy landings were a red herring.

Allied casualties were light: the Canadians lost about a third of their total of casualties at Dieppe in 1942. The total loss was about 2,500. Inland from Gold beach, Trooper Kenneth Ewing, a tank driver of the Sherwood Rangers, needed to relieve himself and crouched in a hedge. In it already was a German. As Ewing prepared to defecate on him Fritz decided to surrender and poked the ranger on the bum.

Ewing leapt up in terror and ran headlong into the field and tripped over his trousers pursued by Fritz with his hands up. 'Kamerad! Kamerad!' he called out desperately.

Late on D-Day Major Richard Gosling, 147 Field Regiment (Essex Yeomanry), Royal Artillery, came across a pillbox at the back of Gold. Inside there was a letter: 'Hans, chérie, je vous attendrai derrière le pillbox à six heurs du soir le six Juin, Madeleine.'

Gosling and his men waited around hopefully but Madeleine never turned up.

The 8th Battalion of the Royal Irish Hussars experienced something similar inland from Juno beach on 9 June. Laagered in a field for a day they espied some French girls wearing German field boots and staring inquisitively over a hedge. These newcomers could be killjoys but, on the other hand, there could be new opportunities.

On Sword beach HQ, 1st Special Service Brigade were greeted with a hail of bullets and shells. Piper Bill Millin, however, was ready to do his duty. 'What tune would you like me to play, sir?' he asked the CO.

'Well, let's see,' pondered the colonel. '"The Road to the Isles", I think.'

'Would you like me to move up and down, sir?'

'Yes, yes. March up and down. That'll be lovely.'

Millin trudged past the tide washing up bodies. Those still living were flat on their stomachs: the only one upright was Millin.

'Listen, boy,' advised a prostrate sergeant, 'what are you f***ing playing at, you mad bastard? You're attracting every f***ing German in France. All of 'em knows we're here with the f***ing noise you're making.'

But Millin was generally appreciated by the 1st Special Service and they sang along with *The Road to the Isles*.

The Free French also landed on Sword beach – very proudly. Each soldier wore the Cross of Lorraine and their shoulder titles read 'L'audace et toujours de l'ardour'. Many of them were Dunkirk veterans, including their commander, Philippe Kieffer. He led his men into Ouistrehan at the mouth of the River Orne and took special delight in capturing the heavily defended Cassino, where he had lost a fortune before the war.

Captain Patrick Hennessey and his tank crew (13th and 18th Hussars) were less fortunate. Their tank was knocked out on Sword and they had to sit and fume as other tanks swept gaily past them.

'Hard luck, sir,' called someone from one of them and threw over a tin of self-heating mulligatawny soup, which was actually quite welcome because the stranded crew were shivering in the pouring rain.

Sergeant Desmond O'Neill was a cameraman with the Army Film and Photographic Unit. He spotted an absolute gem for a picture. Two very small infantrymen marched cheerfully by with an extremely tall, and terrified, prisoner. They stopped and posed for O'Neill and the result is shown in the photograph on p. 168.

Eric Ashcroft (South Lancashires) lay in the dunes on Sword watching a procession of ants going about their daily business. 'Goodness me,' he ruminated, 'they don't care about the war.'

Back at home, a lady in Torquay received a birthday card from her soldier husband in the second post on 6 June. It was not her birthday so she knew the Second Front had begun. Two elderly ladies in Hastings watched planes roaring overhead all day whilst convoys of troops clogged the streets of the town.

'It's been a funny sort of day, hasn't it, dear?' remarked one to the other.

'Yes, dear. I quite expected it to rain after lunch but it never did.'

Advance

The force on Gold reached the outskirts of Bayeux by midnight on the 6th. The main obstacle to progress proved to be the enormous Normandy hedges with deep ditches on either side. The invaders had been practising on the smaller English hedges and ditches.

There was some enemy opposition. A lance-corporal of the 5th Battalion of the East Yorkshire Regiment was shot in the backside on 7 June. He yanked down his trousers and there was blood everywhere. He feared the worst, but a pal, a real pal, after close examination, reassured him that everything was intact.

'It must 'ave gone straight up yer arse,' he suggested.

Also on that day, there was bad news and good news for Trooper Geoff Ferdie. His tank crew walked over to a deserted-looking barn and found an enemy Tiger tank inside, along with its crew. The bad news was that Ferdie and co. were taken prisoner, but the good news was that it was the lap-gunner's 21st birthday and the Panzer crew produced some bottles of wine.

'We cannot let that past uncelebrated,' said the Tiger commander.

By 12 June the battle for Caen was in full flow. Hitler still waited for the 'real' invasion, in the Pas de Calais, following Garbo's information. Lieutenant Richard Todd (7th Paras) was battling with the 21st Panzer Division outside the city near Le Port. The paras' fire had wrecked the church and killed the German defenders in it. Todd went into the church, which had no roof, and removed his helmet to pray. He was a devout Irish Catholic boy.

A few days after D-Day young Lionel King was in Grange Park Road (the V1s had started falling on London) in Leyton watching a long procession of tanks passing by. One carried a large notice: 'No leave, no babies' and onlookers were left wondering whether that was bad news or good news. Lionel didn't have a clue what it meant.

SIXTEEN

The Second Front

The battle for Caen

The 2nd SS Panzer Division was ordered north from Toulouse on 6 June. It reached Normandy on 18 June. They had started off by road but 'Hilaire' (George Starr) blew up its petrol dumps and so the heavy tanks took to the railway. 'Edgar' (Baron Philippe de Gunzbourg) blew up the railway bridge.

The Panzers veered east but 'Nestor' (Jaques Poitier) and his accomplices started blowing up the actual tanks. It also did not help much that the division's top-secret Ultra signals complaining about Hilaire, Edgar and Nestor were read at Bletchley Park.

The battle for Caen and the Falaise Gap was meanwhile in full swing and the Desert Rats were once more in the thick of the action. In the struggle for Villers-Bocage an 13 June, men of the 1st and 7th Queen's Brigade looked down on a Tiger in the street below from a first floor shop window and discussed ways of disabling it.

They had just decided on throwing a blanket soaked in petrol on top of it when it sprang into life and came straight through the shop window. The brigade beat a hasty retreat out of the tradesman's entrance.

Alan Moorehead was also in the village on the same day, but hopes of tripe and escallop à la Normandie, a local speciality, at the 'Vieux Puits' restaurant were dashed. It had closed for the season.

Around 500,000 Allied troops were in Normandy by 20 June but the German High Command still regarded the bridgehead as a diversion and awaited the proper invasion. No one liked to disagree with Adolf (or Garbo). Reserves entering Bayeux were amused with the notice on the bridge: 'Defense de pisser dans la Rivière.'

On 16 June Gordon Johnson of the 5th Royal Tank Regiment was wounded at Villers Bocage near Caen. At this moment he was in the vicinity of the American forces and was thus taken to an American military hospital in Worcester. An American general came round handing out purple hearts. He arrived at Gordon's bedside.

'On behalf of the President of the United States of America and the people of ...'

Gordon, not usually disposed to interrupting generals, nevertheless felt he had to say something at this point. 'I think there must be some mistake ...' he began to say.

'A goddam Limey!' snapped the general, snatching back the medal.

Sergeant George Stimpson came across an abandoned tank in Villers-Bocage, also on 16 June. He drove it back to HQ and handed it back to the crew who had obviously scarpered when the going got too hot to handle. But first he removed the compo rations and brewing-up kit.

'But, Sergeant, where's our rations and brewing-up kit?' demanded the tank commander.

'Where did you leave the tank, sir?' asked George. There was no answer to that and Stimson and his crew enjoyed extra mixed fruit pudding and a good strong brew.

The battle for Villers Bocage raged on as Private Buggs of the 1st and 5th Queen's became a hero. Not only did he bring all the bumf for the adjutant and the post on 19 June, but also several gallons of fresh milk which he had deftly removed from local cows on the way through. The adjutant even suggested that Buggs should be mentioned in despatches but the CO pointed out that there was no provision for heroic milking under intense enemy fire in King's Regulations.

It had been raining cats and dogs for five days. 'We're in the wrong war,' remarked Trooper Hewison. 'This must be 1917.'

Cherbourg was under siege on 25 June but Field Marshal von Rundstedt was still of the view that the (non-existent) First United

States Army Group would pounce in the Pas de Calais region before long. On the fall of Cherbourg on 29 June both von Rundstedt and Rommel asked Hitler how he imagined the war could still be won. But their armies fought valiantly to hold on to Caen and the Falaise Gap despite ferocious assaults from land, sea and air (HMS *Rodney* bombarded the city on 8 July).

Garson Kanin was filming it all for General Eisenhower. Taking a break, he visited a British slit trench toilet. A corporal sat at a small table dishing out to each customer exactly three sheets of toilet paper. Kanin regarded this as inadequate.

'May I have another sheet, please,' he requested politely. 'I'm making this film for General Eisenhower.'

But to the corporal orders were orders. 'No, sir, you'll find the three easily sufficient, sir. It's one up, one down and one polish.'

Captain Charles A. Gates was the commander of the first all-black American tank group in combat – 761 Tank Battalion. General Patton had originally not much time for black soldiers but changed his mind after seeing them in the battle for Caen. He came round to congratulate them, insofar as General Patton ever praised anybody.

'When you see those Kraut s.o.bs don't spare the ammunition,' he advised. The black soldiers cheered enthusiastically: here was a white man encouraging them to blast hell out of other white men.

Black Americans were especially welcomed in Brittany where the citizens enjoyed jazz (they had buried their records of Louis Armstrong and Duke Ellington to prevent them falling into the hands of the enemy).

'M'ssieu, ze music, le jazz,' cried out a native in ecstasy, hugging and kissing his black heroes. Private Timuel Black now seriously considered settling down in this friendly, non-racist region for good.

Trooper W. Hewison (1st Royal Tank Regiment) was in reserve on the evening of 3 July when he heard pipes playing. He crossed several fields and discovered the lone piper, a captain of the Scottish Yeomanry. He played a lament and a Strathspey and a march for Hewison, who then requested *Mushlocky Bridge*.

Listening reverently to the tones Hewison remarked, 'I'm sure if I ever go to Hades I'll find a Scotsman playing a reel round the Devil.'

By 4 July Caen was flattened by bombardment apart from the whorehouse in the centre. The 2nd Canadian Road Construction Company abandoned the idea of trying to build a road through the rubble and created a beautiful bypass, knocking down everything in its path; a planner's paradise.

General Patton addressed a great throng of his men on 6 July. 'I'm proud to be here to fight beside you. Now let's cut the guts out of the Kraut and get the hell on to Berlin. And when we get to Berlin I am going to personally shoot that paper-hanging goddamned son-of-a-bitch just like I would some snake.'

Operation Cobra

General Patton sped off in his official jeep. Inspired by this his army broke out of the Normandy bridgehead by August in Operation Cobra, helped by Montgomery's breakthrough between Caen and Falaise. Co-operation between infantry and tanks had never seen a better day: the infantry looked upon tank men as dwarfs, or, at least, contortionists, or deformed in some way.

The 5th Royal Inniskilling Dragoon Guards came out from England on 28 July to replace the formidable 8th Hussars. A Hussar stuck his head out of a tank and surveyed the newcomers.

'What mob are you?' he asked quite politely.

'Skins.'

'Never heard of 'em,' grunted the Hussar, disappearing into the dark and oily depths of his machine.

Trooper Hewison was interested in girls as well as pipes. French females had generally recovered from the loss of their German boyfriends. Lucille with the lovely blue eyes owned a shop in Bayeux. Just one glance and Hewison was her slave. He offered to buy her shop. Actually, bartering was in full swing: Hewison was asked for two tins of sardines for a tub of butter.

'Christ, you must be joking,' he said to the madame. 'How about two eggs for two tins of sardines.' Madame was agreeable; she was short of sardines but loaded up with butter.

Captain Mickie O'Brien, commanding Y Troop of 47 (RM) Commando, won the MC (Military Cross) on 23 July east of Sallenelles. His valour involved crossing a minefield under intense fire in order to rescue wounded men. When asked later how he had coped with the horror and destruction he referred to a strong sense of fatalism and no imagination.

Later he reached Fécamp and liberated too much of the town's Benedictine. His CO threatened him with an orchiectomy (with a blunt knife), partial garrotting and the firing squad.

Hitler ordered a counter-attack to cut off the American forces around Cherbourg on 6 August, but this was stopped by the American defence of Mortain. General Patton came round again and visited Flying Officer Rahmer and his huge Mustang. Patton looked the very young man up and down: 'Boy, how old are you?'

'I'm twenty, sir.'

'Do you fly that goddamn airplane?'

'Yes, sir.'

'Son-of-a-bitch,' screamed the general and sped off once more in his jeep. He surveyed the scenes of war desolation stretching on all sides. 'Compared to war,' he yelled at his aide, 'all other forms of human endeavour shrink to insignificance.'

'God, how I love it!' he intoned with great emotion. Later he gave a rocket to an officer who had covered up the insignia on his helmet.

'Inexcusable!' he screamed. 'Do you want to give your men the idea that the enemy is dangerous?'

Dead Horse Alley

The Wehrmacht was now in rapid retreat from the Cherbourg peninsula, suffering carnage along Dead Horse Alley. The Americans reached the Atlantic coast south and west of the Falaise Gap and the Loire at Nantes on 13 August. Patton was highly exuberant but he hated Monty almost as much as the enemy.

'We've got elements in Argenton,' he pointed out to General Bradley, his superior. 'Let me go on to Falaise and we'll drive the British into the sea for another Dunkirk.'

'Nothing doing,' said Bradley grimly. He knew Patton meant it.

Operation Tractable drove the Allies on to Falaise and swept them on towards Paris. Smokey the kitten was in the midst of the Normandy campaign with 5th Royal Tank Regiment (RTR). Later, in Holland, he deserted.

'Sensible cat,' reckoned Gordon Johnson, the wireless operator who had brought Smokey out from England. Near Livarot, south-east of Caen, on 17 August, he spotted a tiny Jock lugging a heavy wireless set and a very large goose – slung over his shoulder. Gordon offered to give him a hand with the goose, not without ulterior motive. Jock was not having any truck with this. 'I'll manage,' he replied politely. 'These f***ing French hens are only half the size of a good Scottish one.'

The battle for Paris

On 20 August 5th RTR were 5 miles to the west of Livarot, crossing the strategic bridge at Fervaques. Deliriously happy citizens climbed all over Norman Smith's tank. Norman and Bert Divell had already finished off the commander's whisky: now their civilian visitors brought plenty of Calvados. Norman recovered consciousness in a field the next morning with a headache reaching down to his boots. German forces fled from Paris.

There was a further Allied invasion between Cannes and Toulon. Fritz evacuated southern France. On 26 August General de Gaulle walked in triumph down the Champs Élysée and Malcolm Muggeridge, an intelligence officer, arrested P.G. Wodehouse because of broadcasts he had made to the USA in 1941 whilst in internment in Germany. There was no accusation that he was another Lord Haw-Haw and eventually they let him go, and he went straight to the USA.

'Great Swan Up'

From late August to 2 September there was the 'Great Swan Up' to Ghent and 11th RTR ran out of petrol in the village square of Mazingarbe, near Lens. The patrons of a nearby bistro offered loud advice and free drinks. Trooper Hewison was in his element: Belgian girls were even prettier than the French ones.

Belgium and beyond

Ghent was captured on 4 September and Gordon Johnson (5th RTR) was presented with a baby to hold as the citizens celebrated wildly. Gordon, through local generosity, had to make a hasty flight to the public toilets where he found a German hiding with a rifle. He only wanted to '*Kamerad*', and offered his rifle, yet Gordon's problem was that he needed to get his trousers down as rapidly as possible.

'You – hold, me – shit,' he improvised.

The dancing in the streets lasted all night to the sounds of illegal recordings of the Andrews Sisters on wireless short wave. 'Don't you sit under the apple tree with anyone else but me,' they crooned over the ancient cobbles.

Highly skilled Belgian chefs cooked bully beef, tinned fruit pudding and *pommes frites*. There were also gallons of local brew, and German wine and cigars marked 'Fur Deutsche Wehrmacht'. Later, there was English tea, hidden carefully for five years by the Flemings.

In Brussels Ron Davies was out with friends at Maxims, a nightclub. After a few beers he sung *Pennies from Heaven* to an appreciative audience. The local radio announced that Germany had surrendered and the celebrations were even wilder in London, with taxis full of singing soldiers (as reported in the *Daily Herald*, 6 September). Anyway, it was a decent rehearsal for the real thing.

It was a false dawn but an American soldier, Charles D. Hiller, entered the Fatherland on 10 September, and Dunkirk came under reverse siege on the 16th – sweet revenge.

Holland

In the calamity of Arnhem (17–26 September) Norman Dicken of 10th PARA pretended to be dead as a line of enemy soldiers moved towards him near the village of Wolfhege, where the paras were trying to hang on in the pocket around Oosterbeck. One of the Jerries stumbled over Norman and, for some reason, thought it was very funny. They all joined in the merriment, including Norman. They helped him to his feet, gave him a drink and carefully cleaned the blood off his face.

Gordon Johnson's tank was parked in a Dutch village on 11 October. It was freezing cold and when the tank rolled off the following morning the tracks were plastered with condoms. It had been parked outside the Bordello. Trooper Hewison was resting – he needed rests between one girlfriend and the next – between Het Wilt and Ravenstein when he became aware of the local hostility to girls who had 'collaborated' with the enemy. He managed to rescue the best-looking one, who was called Reik, and collaborated with her. He was also still active in marketing – Yankee pants, officers' raincoats, towels and fags.

A tank went into a dyke near Doornhoek Bridge. The ever-smiling Armoured Recovery Team – Sergeant Davids and Trooper Sharpe, rolled up.

'Swimming, are we, sir?' Davidson greeted the commander.

It was all one-way traffic in November: Strasbourg was captured on the 23rd and Metz on the 25th. By December much of the 7th Armoured Division (Desert Rats) had served their two years in foreign climes and could go back home or take extended leave before returning. The Queen's Brigade had lost so many men it was broken up. The Brigadier presented every man with fifty cigarettes and there was a big send-off party. The closing ceremony was at the Menin Gate in Ypres. The Regimental Serjeant Major (RSM) was surrounded by some tearful citizens as he spoke to his troops.

'Which of you bastards flogged this man a TCV?' he demanded fiercely (a TCV was a troop-carrying vehicle).

It was the coldest winter the Dutch could remember. 5th RTR looked like penguins they had so much gear on. Their gauntlets came only in one size – bunch-of-bananas size. They still got frostbite.

Ron Davies fell ill and spent some weeks in Nijmegen Hospital. Trying to return to his unit he got hopelessly lost but was given accommodation for the night by a nice Dutch family. The food was excellent and the bed was comfortable – except for the fact that it harboured thousands of bugs.

Not wishing to upset these kindly people Ron crept out to a barn. However, in the middle of the night, he needed to go to the toilet, choosing an adjacent field. He had nothing with which to wipe his bottom but, searching in his pockets, he found a scrap of paper fit for purpose.

It was only when he was about a mile away from the house next morning when he realised that the 'scrap of paper' had been a 50-gilder note, worth about £5, a tidy sum in those days. So he returned to the scene of action and retrieved it from the frozen heap.

The Battle of the Bulge

For once Allied intelligence failed to keep ahead of the game, by not detecting enemy plans for an Ardennes offensive in December. From 16 December the enemy drove the Allies back about 50 miles, almost reaching the River Meuse at Dinant by Christmas. The advance was assisted by a special group of thirty-three German commandos who all spoke fluent English and were disguised as Allied soldiers.

The deception caused widespread confusion and anxiety: General Bradley was accosted no less than three times by suspicious sentries. He had to prove he was American by knowing the capital of Illinois, the guard between the centre and the tackle on a line of scrimmage in American football and the current spouse of Betty Grable.

Richard 'Red' Prendergast, a mortarman, was captured in this Battle of the Bulge. In the POW camp it was so cold the guards refused to stay outside and substituted a big, vicious German shepherd dog. It was stationed inside a 40ft fence with coils of barbed wire on top of it. The prisoners shot it and cooked it.

'It was just like T-bone,' reckoned Red. The guards were completely mystified by the complete disappearance of their guard dog. Not a hair could be found.

The Battle of the Bulge was more or less over by Christmas. Major-General Anthony McAuliffe held on with his American army in Bastogne. When invited to surrender by Jerry he sent a cryptic message – 'Nuts'. They could not understand it so he despatched something more specific – 'Go to hell'.

Meanwhile, Lieutenant Gerald Lascelles's batman continued his endless search for pianos in any town or village they entered so that his officer could perform on it. In Braeksittard Trooper B.L. Roberts gathered up all the tools of the local cobbler, who had gone away, and mended everyone's footwear, even their clogs. He became known as 'Robart the Schooner Maker'.

Captain Ray Wax was also able to resume his impresario activities. He had a piano but needed someone to play it. A shy, slim volunteer stepped forward.

'What's your name, son?' asked Wax.

'Dave Brubeck, sir,' he replied.

Previously, in Paris, Ray Wax missed the Victory Parade as he was in Galerie Lafayette purchasing silk scarves and perfume. Later, he tried to get into a posh restaurant but it had been requisitioned by the Maquis, so Ray toddled off to an establishment which did well out of the black market.

'It became one of those great marathon Hemingway kind of nights,' he recalled. 'In this bar, Chez Mam, at 1 a.m., I was laid out on a f***ing piano singing "Hurrah for the flag of the free".'

Ray published a newspaper for the American troops – *The Daily Belch*. He deliberately put in a lot of items about the Eastern Front and the progress of the Russians. 'You couldn't convince a GI anybody was out fighting the f***ing war but him,' he explained.

Meanwhile, Lieutenant Elliot Johnson and his company were crossing the River Aare on inflatable rubber boats and the order of the night was caution and silence. But Private Bond had kept a lot of the hard stuff from Normandy and it was a good opportunity to have a good slug or two of it.

'Row! Row! Row your boat!' he sang raucously and an enemy mortar opened up.

It was a different story crossing Nijmegen Bridge (although the troops were also under intense fire). Captain Warburton looked and sounded like Noel Coward in a war film. 'Well, there's nothing for it, chaps,' he said bravely. 'We just have to go on.'

A faint raspberry could be heard in the background.

SEVENTEEN

Elsewhere
June-December 1944

Italy

On 4 June the Americans were in Rome. Alex Bowlby was resting in a field selected by the intelligence officer as a safe haven. They had just got into their cosy, ready-to-wear cocoons of blankets when the shells started landing. The field was registered by enemy artillery.

Bowlby was thus glad to get back to Regello still in one piece and celebrated his good fortune by offering a shabby Italian shuffling along a couple of fags. 'Thanks, mate,' said the 'Itie', 'can't I 'ave the whole f***ing packet?'

This deserter proved to be a dealer in khaki-drill trousers, 'tens of thousands' of which had been lost in the Battle for Rome. They were very popular with Italian peasants.

Bowlby's girlfriend, Violetta, knew his regiment was on the move again before he did. She had more military intelligence than rank and file. They duly moved north the next day, along with some ack-ack wallahs, including an effeminate-looking private with blonde hair and answering to the name 'Goldilocks'. Private Meadows pretended to be nice to him and ascertained the fact that Goldilocks was a tap dancer in civvy street.

'You couldn't 'ave picked a better platoon,' Meadows confided. 'We're all musical 'ere. My friend Page 'ere plays the violin smashing, don't you, Charlie, mate?'

'Do you really?' asked Goldilocks eagerly.

'Course 'e does,' confirmed Meadows. 'I cut the gut out of a cat for the strings.' The platoon howled with glee but Goldilocks burst into tears.

'You horrid beasts!' he cried. 'I'll show you, I'll show you!'

'Don't mind them,' Private Humphreys tried to console him by putting a friendly arm round the young private. 'They're only taking the piss.'

The platoon turned to studying some Jerry leaflets – propaganda which had been fired over. They contained a picture of a GI lifting a girl's skirt underneath a spreading chestnut tree. The story was provided underneath the picture: 'A girl in Maidstone was walking home when an American soldier asked if he could join her.'

The young maiden took up the sad tale: 'He said there was a lovely view from some bush. We went over and sat down. He opened a can of beer, pulled me into the bushes, inned me and outed me, wiped his tallywock on my skirt, pissed in the beer and walked away whistling "God save the King".'

"You Americans are sooo different!"

'Meanwhile, Tommy, at home …' German propaganda shot over Allied lines in Italy, 1944.

On 18 June Bowlby was near Perugia and swam in the Tiber. His pal, Rifleman Fletcher, went under water for some time. He surfaced: 'I've lorst me teeth!' he cried out in anguish. 'I've lorst me teeth!' False teeth were an important part of the Second World War.

They all fished around for his nashers but with no success. He reported sick and was sent down the line for three days of 'rest and recuperation'. How this was designed to restore his dentures only the British army would know.

Perugia was taken on 20 June and Lieutenant Philip Brutton (3rd Battalion of the Welsh Guards), in nearby San Marco, was mobbed and kissed by happy civilians. He wasn't really all that pleased with such hilarity. 'They were all unshaven men,' he complained.

Another of Bowlby's friends, the Irishman O'Connor, was granted leave in Rome on the grounds that he was seeking an audience with the Pope.

Major Edward Prebble had left Goldilocks' unit – the Artillery Reinforcement Department – because it was a bit of a dead-end for an ambitious officer. He had seen an advert for an 'entomologist'. Prebble didn't have a clue what this meant but it sounded different so he applied.

He was posted to the Medical School of Hygiene at Benvento and arrived in the middle of a lecture. He was immediately directed to examine a slide through a microscope by a rather stroppy sergeant.

'I can't see a thing,' he admitted.

'You've still got the cover on – sir,' said the sergeant.

Prebble was apparently supposed to be studying a mosquito – an 'exotic' mosquito, which had never been spotted in Italy. Having succeeded in finding the creature under the microscope he was then despatched to Taranto as assistant adjutant general (mosquitos), armed with an armband, a large magnifying glass, a butterfly net, a frying pan, a truck and a driver. His job was to keep down the incidence of malaria – and he was quite successful at it.

Back in Naples, in October, so many jeeps were being unloaded at the docks that the going rate was a bottle of whisky for a jeep. The 3rd Welsh Guards had seven vehicles with the same registration number. The task of the officer in charge of transport was to make sure they weren't in the same place at the same time.

Alex Bowlby was in the Base Hospital at Bari at this time. An important senior officer came to visit his ward and the senior soldier there bawled out an order to the prostrate patients. 'Lie to attention!' Bowlby pushed his arms straight by his sides and his legs together and straight. It made a change from eluding the nymphomaniac nurse who whipped off his bedclothes at strategic moments.

At the front the 19th New Zealand Armoured Regiment crossed the River Rubicon on 11 October, which was an unmistakeable message to Adolf Hitler. Klaus Huebner was not celebrating, however, because food was in short supply. A cow had been shot but it had to be fried in Barbasel shaving cream. Huebner took some of the liver and had diarrhoea for a week. He was a doctor of an American battalion and found that caring for his men and dealing with the raving trots was a difficult combination.

Rome was as dangerous as the front. Deserters enjoyed nocturnal muggings and armed robberies. Philip Brutton, on leave, carried around a pocket-sized biretta. Brutton was hoping to get into a swish restaurant – Alfredo's – but he was refused entry so he and his Italian girlfriend pressed on to Osso's. You still had to be someone to get in. Kinka, the girl, said she was a well-known ENSA soprano from Swansea. The receptionist was not sure.

'Well, do you want me to sing?' demanded this resourceful lady – her version of 'Swansea' not bad. There was a nod from the head waiter, who had worked at the Savoy. He gave the couple a conspiratorial wink and led them to a good table.

Doodlebugs and rockets

On 13 June six people were killed in Grove Road, Bow by a V1 'flying bomb' (Vergeltung 1 – 'Release 1') at 4.25 a.m. As far as Londoners were concerned, they were 'Bumble Bombs' – at first. Then they were 'Buzz Bombs' by 25 June and 'Doodlebugs' by 2 July. On this day one of them hit a house in Kenton Gardens, Harrow. George Beardmore, a Mass Observationist, was the local Senior Billeting Officer and one of his jobs was to keep track of where bombed-out survivors were.

Two sisters lived at Kenton Gardens. Beardmore was told that one, Jessie, was staying with friends in Wembley, while the other, Mary, had just arrived home on leave from the WAAF. No one knew where she was and the Heavy Rescue Squad spent a fruitless night trying to find her in the rubble.

The next day Jessie called into George's office.

'Do you know where your sister is?' he asked.

'What sister? I'm an only child.'

'But where's Mary?'

'Oh, I see. I'm called Mary in the WAAF and Jessie at home.'

The only people not laughing were the Heavy Rescue Squad. George held a public meeting later in the day. When he'd finished he asked, 'Any questions?'

'Yes – where's Mary?' called a wag from the back of the room.

The government ordered that obituaries for folk killed by Doodlebugs must be limited to three per postal district in order not to encourage the Germans or raise alarm and despondency. They were liable to go off in any direction from the launching pads: one nearly hit Hitler's HQ in Soissons on 17 June. But they still accounted for 1,935 civilians within sixteen days.

Lionel King in Leyton watched as the spotter on the roof of a firm, Jenkins's, threw himself off the building when he spotted a V1 coming straight for him. According to Lionel, he 'only' broke both legs.

David Card, another young lad, scrumping in an orchard in Woolwich, also observed a plunging Doodlebug. It struck the farmhouse. What he remembered most clearly were the thousands of chicken feathers floating down.

On 30 June 198 people died in the Strand. On 4 July the first precision air attack on the launching sites resulted in the destruction of over 2,000 flying bombs at St Leu-d'Esserent near Paris, and thousands went at Nucourt on 10 July.

An editorial in the *Sunday Express* for 5 July observed that 'it must be very irksome to some of our sentimentalists that they cannot offer a cup of tea to a flying bomb'. There were also nice pictures of Monty with two pups christened 'Hitler' and 'Rommel'. The editorial was of the view that this was not fair on the dogs.

Another Mass Observationist, Muriel Green, lived and worked in North London. She recalled lots of bangs on 28 July. At each bang everyone in her office dropped flat before finally looking at each other and bursting out laughing. They were amused at how daft they must have looked.

Hundreds of thousands of children were once more evacuated from the capital – more, in fact, than in the Blitz in 1940. My sister and I went to our granny's bungalow in Wickford, Essex, and on the night we arrived a Doodlebug hit the field next to us, badly damaging the cabbages. Wisely, our parents decided that it made more sense moving us away from the V1 sites rather than nearer them. We travelled to other relations in Glastonbury, Somerset.

Before then, we had plenty of opportunities to study the V1. A theory developed that if its engine cut out at about 30° east of your current position you were in trouble (this theory was unable to embrace those which did not cut out at all but just came straight down). But anything still buzzing over your head was an overshoot – for you, at least. If you saw one, as I did on a number of occasions, it wasn't going to hit you and you could observe it with a sort of detached fascination.

German 'spies' were transmitting misinformation about where they were falling. Those hitting central London were reported as falling in the countryside to the north. They were not falling in the south of London, the spies said. As a result, the range was shifted south – good news for Tower Bridge but not Croydon. Subsequently, many hit the suburbs and countryside to the south of London and Croydon suffered 142 bombs and the loss of more than 1,000 houses. Bromley, Bexley and Orpington also fared badly. This was an early example of the application of the NIMBY principle.

By the end of August the RAF and the ack-ack had got the measure of the V1s, and of ninety-seven fired on 28 August only four fell on London. A newspaper headline of 8 September read 'It's Over!' So we came back to the Isle of Dogs. Waiting for us were around 1,000 11-ton rockets which could travel at 4,000mph (not to mention thousands more Doodlebugs dropped by Heinkels flying over the North Sea). If you want to appreciate the size of a V2 rocket go and look at the one in the Imperial War Museum.

On the night of the headline 'It's Over!', rockets fell on Chiswick and Epping.

A V2 was a vastly different proposition from a V1. All you heard was 'CRUMP' – and not all that loud, actually. At least if you heard 'CRUMP' you were safe. 'CRUMP' was miles away. A school friend of mine took back his dad's cider bottles (you got twopence per bottle) to a pub in Poplar one lunchtime. I never saw him again. By the end of October there were about four 'CRUMPS' a day.

It was a total lottery who suffered. Ilford was the unluckiest borough, followed by West Ham, Barking, Dagenham, Walthamstow, Finchley and Stepney. But not the Isle of Dogs. I was pretty relieved the spies didn't report that they were all falling in the Essex countryside.

The last V1 attack in 1944 was on Christmas Eve. Inside the warheads were Christmas cards sent by British POWs to their loved ones.

In the air

The RAF had continued to bomb V1 and V2 launching sites. From one raid Wing Commander John Grey, in his Lancaster, managed to get back to Manston on one engine, but the control tower refused him permission to land on the runway because they were testing out a Gloster Meteor jet plane. The wing commander was obliged to come down on the grass.

He played snooker with his crew that night. 'You're a bloody good pilot,' observed Larry Sutherland, 'but you're a bloody awful snooker player.' During the night he crept into Squadron Leader Sidney Pattinson's room and cut off half his handlebar moustache. There was no respect for rank.

Allied bombers continued to attack German cities, industry and communications. Potentially war-winning targets were synthetic oil installations. Bomber Command also had to cover Italy and the Second Front.

There was little glamour back at base, either. Sergeant James Hampton of 76 Squadron remembered bare and cold Nissen huts.

They had burnt all the furniture in the stove after the coke ran out. There was one washhouse for 400 air crew, sixteen tin bowls and a few showers offering tepid water. But this was 'home'. Officers had a room and a WAAF to make their beds.

In the few hours off duty officers and other ranks continued to try and forget all about it (even wing commanders – John Voyce and choir could offer a decent rendering of *Please Don't Burn Our Shithouse Down*). The bomber boys at Elsenham had nights out at the Berkeley pub in Scunthorpe. The bus called for them at 10 p.m., and off it went crammed full of airmen crammed full of (weak) beer, singing several different ditties at the same time. They dropped off the WAAFs at their camp and then took the opportunity to tumble out and urinate up the fence.

Crew could try sex with 'saloon-bar sirens': some did, some didn't and some teased. Alternatively, for the more energetic, there was adventure in muddy fields ('scrub-riding') – diving into ditches, crossing planks over streams (or falling in them) and crashing into the perimeter fence around the mental asylum for air crew.

On 7 June, 210 Squadron were attacking enemy positions west of Caen. It was on the way back that Wallace McIntosh had real fun, shooting down two Heinkels and three night fighters. 'Quiet trip' Wallace wrote in his log. At base a congratulatory postagram arrived from Sir Arthur 'Bomber' Harris, chief of Bomber Command.

Their own celebrations consisted of a trip to the pictures in Skegness. They joined in a largely RAF audience in jeering at the story of a handful of smooth-talking Yanks defeating a large force of Fritzes.

On 12 August 207 Squadron was stood down and didn't waste a second before scattering to pubs all over the East Midlands. However, later that night, they were rounded up by service police.

'All aircraft crew from 207 Squadron out now!'

There was going to be a last-minute raid on the Falaise Pocket. The vast bulk of 207 could hardly stand let alone fly a Lancaster. But back at Spilsby, Command managed to get together six makeshift crews. They went over and completed the mission, along with other Lancasters, Halifaxes, Stirlings and Mosquitos. On their safe return 207 personnel collapsed into bed, somewhat sobered up.

Squadron Leader Basil 'stap me' Stapleton, in command of 247 Squadron, acquired his nickname from the cartoon strip 'Just Jake', where the main character always said 'stap me' if he spotted a nice girl. The squadron was flying from advanced airstrips in Normandy in August.

Stapleton, like so many other Allied servicemen, became partial to Calvados. Apart from drinking it, he also discovered that it was handy for lighting paraffin lamps and also his Zippo lighter.

The logo on his plane was a burning swastika with the label 'Excreta Thermo'. He crash-landed on 23 December and was taken prisoner and sent to Stalag Luft I. A fellow prisoner described the Spitfire as 'beautiful and frail yet agile, potent and powerful'.

'Stap me,' gasped Stapleton. 'I've always wanted to meet a woman like that.'

Johnny Byrne's first mission on 2 November was to 'Happy Valley', otherwise known as Düsseldorf. He was wireless operator onboard Lancaster 'Press-on Regardless' (550 Squadron, Killingholm, Lincolnshire).

Byrne had recently passed his initiation ceremony, during which he was blindfolded and ordered to down a tankard of bitter. Before he had finished, the blindfold was whipped off and he could see the 'turds' nestling in the bottom of the glass. They were actually made of parkin (sticky ginger cake).

Later that evening Flying Officer 'Val' Valerio, a popular accordionist, dropped his instrument to his chest when seated, threw his legs in the air, lit a match and applied it to his bottom and broke wind. A 5ft sheet of blue flame shot out from his posterior and the WAAFs scattered in all directions.

There were similar prevalent problems in the air, including 21 Officer Training Unit, based at Moreton-in-Marsh, Gloucestershire and flying Halifaxes.

'Which of you bastards has got gas?' demanded a Halifax pilot fearing the worst after large helpings of baked beans at breakfast.

A special delight back in the mess at Moreton was based on caking someone's feet in a mixture of beer and soot and hoisting him up a wall and across the ceiling. They waited until visitors got drunk before trying it. Visitors stopped drinking after seeing a bloke walk across the ceiling.

At RAF Wickenby there was a mid-upper gunner, a neat, well-groomed man with a lisp and a rather lilting diction. He used scented soaps and frequently dabbed his nose with a tiny silk handkerchief. The presence one night of a group of robust Aussie airmen in the mess boded trouble for Roy. He told them about his nice West End flat.

'Lovely fitted carpets, up to your ankles, dear, and such wonderful pictures on the walls. And I have these simply wonderful pieces of sculpture, done in Scandinavian wood by this marvellous Polish person.'

The Aussies scented fun. 'Do go on, old chap,' one of them encouraged Roy (or Woy).

'Horrid bomb came into my lovely living room!'

There was a shocked chorus of disbelief from Down Under. 'Oh, no, no. Not a bomb! Say it wasn't a bomb!'

Roy's voice became shrill with indignation. 'My dear, it wasn't so much what the bomb did. It was the absolute havoc caused by the fire brigade.'

There were more cries of shock and horror. Someone mimicked Roy's high-pitched dismay: 'Oh dear, how positively dreadful.' He suddenly twigged what they were up to and went pink with anger.

'You're taking the micky,' he cried. 'All you know about are rabbits, and sheep and ... well, kangaroos.'

They tried to calm him down by offering him a drink. This was different. 'Well, I don't mind if I do,' he said, like Colonel Chinstrap of *ITMA*. 'Mine's a large gin and lime, please, if it's all the same to you.'

Roy was nearly at the end of a second tour of duty – over fifty raids – and had been awarded the DFM (Distinguished Flying Medal) and wore a wound stripe.

Women pilots were used in the Air Transport Auxiliary. First Officer Anne Walker took off in a double-winged Walrus from Cowes straight into a cross wind, a hazardous manoeuvre. So fraught, in fact, that she finished up in a haystack with a baker's delivery boy and his bike. Happily, they were unscathed but the loaves had suffered somewhat. The nice lad offered them to

Anne and back at base she and her colleagues enjoyed a great pile of jam sandwiches with very fresh, if slightly soiled and buckled, bread.

Going West

There was another attempt to kill Hitler. This was Operation Valkyrie led by Count von Stauffenberg. The date set was 15 July and so confident of success was General Olbricht that he ordered a reserve army to march on Berlin. Meanwhile, however, the count had moved the date for the assassination – without informing the general. Olbricht's boss, General Fromm, wanted to know why he had sent an army towards Berlin. Olbricht replied that it was a 'surprise exercise'.

It was 20 July when they tried to blow up the Führer in a hut. Von Stauffenberg, not being a suicide bomber, was hurrying on his way several hundred metres away at the time. He took a plane to Berlin and arrived there at 4.30 p.m., just in time to hear that the bomb had missed its target. Undaunted, he carried on and arrested General Fromm, and Major Remer was ordered to surround government offices. Remer, a wise man, refused to do anything until he had spoken to Goebbels, whom Hitler had phoned to say that he was in good health.

Field Marshal von Witzleben broadcast a message at 8.10 p.m:

'The Führer is dead. I have been appointed Commander-in-Chief of the armed forces, and also ...' At this point his voice faded away. Major Remel was awarded the Knight's Cross with Oak Leaves. The best headline in London the next day, according to Frank Edwards, a 32-year-old Mass Observationist, buyer, Home Guardsman and fire-watcher, was: 'Missed Him!'.

But the bomb incident hadn't really done Hitler any good. When General von Vormann visited him on 26 September he described the leader as tired, broken, shuffling and drooped. His hands were shaking. Von Vormann could hardly make out what he was saying. But he did say that he wasn't going to surrender. On 12 December he seemed to be back to his ranting best, declaring to a gathering of generals that he looked forward to the day when Germans could once more be 'solid citizens in grey flannel suits'.

The Americans were 25 miles from Cologne.

In the East

On 31 August equally brave generals, nineteen of them each wearing an Iron Cross, led a parade of 57,000 German soldiers through the streets of Moscow. They were all prisoners, including the generals. On the same day, the Russian army captured Bucharest. In October it was in East Prussia.

That month, George Jellicoe, commanding officer of 8 Commando, cycled 12 miles into Athens with his second in command, Major Ian Patterson. The German invaders had fled from the city. Jellicoe and Patterson came out on the balcony at the Hotel Grande Bretagne and waved like heroes to a vast and rapturously cheering crowd of partisans and citizens.

During the summer months of 1944 thousands of Japanese soldiers were either committing suicide or perishing in banzai charges. British, Indian, Gurkha and American troops invaded Burma on 26 June. On a reef off Saipon Island enemy survivors were beheaded one by one by their officer on 7 July, but an American shot him before he could behead himself.

The re-conquest of New Guinea was completed on 30 July. Here, a Japanese officer was actually captured alive. He was accompanied by a Chinese coolie who was struggling along with several heavy bags containing the lieutenant's spare clothes and food etc. He gravely informed his captors that he was a 'democratic' man and indicated the coolie.

'But he is weak, I am strong,' he explained.

On 21 September American bombers attacked the Philippines and began the invasion of the islands on 20 October. By December kamikaze pilots were causing grave losses. General MacArthur and Admiral Nimitz ordered a news blackout 'in order to prevent panic in the United States'.

News at home late in the year

It was reported that more than 60,000 knives, forks and spoons had been stolen from the London Passenger Transport Board within a year.

An American major in Cambridge mislaid his driver in the blacked-out city and had to call out loudly to attract his attention. Unfortunately, the driver's name was 'Rape'.

Elsewhere in the blackout, a young Somerset housewife, Mrs Anne Lee-Mitchell, came up to London as part of her war work. She was sent to the Duchess Club for officers just behind BBC headquarters. A kind night porter came round to put up her blackout. He was quite chatty, telling her that he could get cheap black-market whisky, that he had nine children and that he was a passionate man.

Anne was then sent to be a station marshal at St Pancras. An anxious mother called out from a train that she had no spoon with which to feed her baby so Anne rushed into the station café, pinched (yet another) spoon and rushed along the platform to get it to the mother, pursued by an irate café owner, fed up with losing so much cutlery.

As Anne sped forth the elastic on her knickers (a common problem on the Home Front) broke and down they came. There was loud applause from passengers, staff and the café owner. But these WVS girls were tough – she completed her mission and took them off and waved them around her head. The acclaim multiplied.

Kenneth Richmond, another Mass Observationist and civil servant in Bridgend, reported a flood in the town on 20 November. The Palais de Dance began sliding into the river and a grand piano hung out of one of the windows. Eventually, it slipped into a watery grave and 'played water music, but not by Handel'.

Pam Ashford, our correspondent in Glasgow, was still filing reports to M.O. in London. She discussed Churchill's speech at the Albert Hall on 24 November. Was he drunk, she wondered? She reckoned he was definitely inebriated during his previous address.

Pam's two elderly friends, Mr and Mrs Fuller, were always well prepared for air raids. She praised their 'prepare to meet thy doom' attitude. They had buckets of water to hand, gas masks on, money secured about their persons and an attaché case containing essentials leant against the front door.

Muriel Green (also a Mass Observationist) was at a New Year's Eve party. The 'Old Year' appeared with a cotton wool beard and a scythe. Then a painted, plywood stork descended from the roof with a 'baby' in a napkin.

Round and about

At Bremerhaven the German navy was building the first 'prefabricated submarine' and in London up went the first prefabricated bungalows ('prefabs') on a few bombed-out sites.

In Colombo, a naval officer bought peanuts from a vendor wrapped in a 'Top Secret' signal.

In Baghdad, Joyce Grenfell was still doing her bit to entertain the forces and writing an equally entertaining diary about it. She met Queen Ali, one of the widows of the King of Hejaz.

'What do you do all day, Your Majesty?' asked Joyce.

'Garden,' replied Her Majesty.

'What are you growing?'

'Oh – not garden. Sit in garden. No wireless, no film, life would be very sad. My Auntie got very sad.'

Her auntie, in fact, had run away with a waiter from Sicily and was disowned by the royal family. They went even further, passing a law declaring that she had never existed. Sadly, the waiter tired of her, he said she had 'no dot'.

EIGHTEEN

North-West Europe 1945

January

The Americans were attacking the Bulge in January but it was hard going. 'There were some unfortunate incidents,' wrote General Patton on 4 January, 'in the shooting of prisoners (I hope we can correct this).' The siege of Bastogne was lifted on 14 January. On the same day the Rifle Brigade was resting at Geleen in Holland but their style was somewhat cramped by the siting of the Regimental Aid Post in the town brothel.

On 15 January an SS colonel remarked to Hitler that they could now travel from the Eastern Front to the Western Front on the Berlin streetcars. Hitler thought this was funny: he must have been losing his grip because surely in his prime he would have had the colonel shot.

Hitler didn't like Jewish jokes: he wrote in *Mein Kampf* that it was impossible to hate someone you laughed at. He was generally selective about jokes. Bert Trautmann, the Manchester City FA Cup Final legend (he played on after breaking his neck) was in the Hitler Youth and he recalled that one could joke about Goering's love of fancy uniforms but not about Adolf's shrill voice and Goebbel's rat-like face.

Lieutenant Bill Kennedy (101st US Airborne Division) was horrified to find some of his men in the village undertaker's shop in Wickersheim, Holland, late on 21 January. They were lying in coffins on their backs with their arms across their chests. Thinking Nazi collaborators had butchered them, he rushed inside in a state of shock and they rose up as a man and screamed with glee. The shop was warm and the coffins comfortable.

The Siegfried Line was assaulted on 30 January. Ron Davies and his mates were collecting fistfuls of very large denominations of German currency – thousands of marks. They threw away the small stuff. But later only notes up to 10 marks remained as legal tender.

February

As the Allied troops approached the River Rhine, Berlin journalists were summoned to a top-level briefing at Tempelhof on 4 February. The mood was sarcastic and the general view was that the top brass were conducting a 'madhouse'. The hacks sat in an enormous glass-walled room listening to high-ranking officials who were 'like parrots in a zoo', 'robots' ridiculously trying to appeal to a patriotism which had long since vanished.

'Hold fast,' lectured one of these puppets. 'Goebbels thinks we are on the brink of victory. We shall win because we must win.'

A lower-ranking official, stuffy, formal and pompous in his ostentatious tie pin, gave the lie to the proceedings by breaking ranks. 'Even the food is a load of shit!' he shouted wildly, but it relieved the tension.

Another meeting on the same day was attended by Stalin, Churchill and Roosevelt in Yalta to discuss what should happen after the war. Stalin wanted British and American bombers to give the Russian advance more support. Churchill already had thoughts about getting Allied forces as far to the East as possible.

At these gatherings the leaders were accompanied by impressive retinues of advisers, interpreters, sentries, typists, clerks and servants. Three toilets were provided in the Vorontsov Palace for the British contingent – one for the prime minister and two between everybody else. Maureen Stuart-Clark, flag lieutenant for Admiral Somerville, recalled detailed discussions about the best bushes in the garden.

'Heil Hitler! Let me present V4 – our best secret weapon yet!' (Cartoon by Stephen Roth)

Indeed, Edward Stebbing (Mass Observationist in Potters Bar) thought that the three great leaders resembled three music-hall comedians.

On 8 February the Canadians drove south from Nijmegen to capture the area between the River Maas and the River Rhine. Warrant Officer Albert Friend was shot down but managed to parachute to safety in Holland and got back to England. He went to get his parachute re-packed.

'Where's the ripcord?' demanded the bloke in the stores.

'Must have lost it,' muttered Albert.

'That'll be seven shillings and sixpence for a new one, please.'

Also around this time, Ron Davies was billeting with the Piones family in Trebeck. The kids asked what he was in the army and Ron told them that he was a corporal but because he had two stripes he was a 'big' corporal. Thereafter, he became 'Der Grosse Caporal'. He had a lot of fun with this nice family – including driving his artillery gun up to the Piones' kitchen window and pointing it at the lady of the house washing up. She thought it was a huge joke.

She wagged a finger at the gun. 'Naughty Caporal Ronnie,' she scolded.

'Naughty Der Grosse Caporal Ronnie,' the children echoed. Ron went back after the war to visit them. 'Der Grosse Caporal' was a big celebrity in the town.

When John Foley, a tank commander, crossed over the German border on 28 February he passed by an old man.

'We on the right road for Berlin, mate?' he called out amicably.

The old man chuckled. 'Berlin? Ja, ja! Gerabe aus!'

'I thought the Germans had no sense of humour,' observed one of John's crew.

'Maybe,' mused his commander, 'but he can remember Germany before Hitler, and probably before the Kaiser, too.'

Ron Davies was near the Rhine at the end of February. He and his chums were trying to get some sleep in a hut when a giant of a Hun, a stormtrooper to boot, burst through the door pointing a machine gun. There was a stampede as he said quietly 'Kamerad.'

When they got their breath back the Jerry led them outside to a whole company of Germans who also wanted to surrender. The only place to incarcerate them was a cellar running alive with rats. Hamelin was just down the road.

'Why not send for the Pied Piper,' suggested a knowledgeable wag.

March–April

The Americans reached the Rhine opposite Düsseldorf on 2 March. All the bridges had gone, except the one at Remagen, the Ludendorf railway bridge, which the defenders failed to blow up in time. Thus

Sergeant Alexander A. Drabik became the first invader to cross the Rhine since Napoleon.

This bridge finally collapsed on 17 March just as enemy frogmen were swimming up river to blow it up. On the 23rd a searchlight with 13 million candlepower ('Monty's Moonlight') enabled British and Canadian troops to cross over at Rees and Wesel and invade the Ruhr, encircled by 3 April. Meanwhile, on 27 March – great news! – Argentina declared war on Germany and Japan.

On 4 April 5th RTR advanced 50 miles and reached a farm in Wagenfeld. Upstairs they made an odd discovery: three beds, each containing four teenage girls.

'Raus! Raus!' ordered George Stimpson, a tank commander.

'They might be soldiers in disguise,' suggested one of his crew. 'They're enrolling boys born in 1929 – it's official.'

'Raus!' ordered George again and indicated that the 'girls' should lift up their nightshirts. George later recalled that this was one of the prettiest sights he'd ever seen.

The 5th RTR were south of Bremen on 8 April. A lap gunner who could speak fluent German got on the blower to the mayor. 'Surrender or we will call up the RAF to blow you to piece,' he threatened fluently.

'We surrender,' pleaded the mayor.

'Probably thinks we've got a direct line to Bomber Harris,' the gunner remarked to George Stimpson.

On 16 April they were in the outskirts of Fallingbostel, on the river near the bridge. Peter Bickersteth was washing his feet in the river when there was an enormous explosion under the bridge and great lumps of concrete came hurtling through the air.

'Get down, skipper, f***ing hell!' yelled the gunner. 'Your feet may need cleaning but the war's not over yet.'

The situation deteriorated into farce: somebody, somewhere, was playing a piano and another tankman fell into a cesspit. He definitely needed cleaning in the river.

In a nearby garage they found a large cabin trunk packed with chocolate, beer and wine. But it took them until the following morning to get hold of a truck and by then the treasure was gone.

Nuremberg, the venue for all the big Nazi rallies, fell on 20 April. Captain Ray Wax was quickly on the scene, hoping to use the opera house for some shows, despite the disadvantage of having a gaping hole in the roof. But the major in charge of it was not co-operative.

'We're guarding sixteen ballerinas,' he pointed out.

'I don't want the f***ing ballerinas,' protested Ray. 'I just want to run shows in it.'

The major relented and let him use half of the building, the half without the ballerinas but with the hole in the roof.

On 18 April the Americans were at Magdeburg, about 90 miles from Berlin, while the Russians were in Frankfurt-on-Oder, about 60 miles from the capital. On the 22nd the 5th RTR fought in the Battle of Buxterhade against 400 German WRENs just out of their beds.

'Unlovely Women!' the *Daily Mirror* called them, but the Desert Rats didn't agree: some of them were quite nice, especially in nightdresses.

Meanwhile, American Lieutenant Albert Kotzebue met a Russian soldier on 25 April near Leckwitz on the Elbe. The Russians were in the outskirts of Berlin on 26 April.

At Stalag Luft III all the guards fled except one old fellow, who sought the prisoners' advice as to what he should do. They liked him: he had been no trouble. 'Get rid of your uniform, Dad, and bugger off home,' advised Lance-Corporal Norman Norris, and bugger off he did.

In Hamburg, the 8th Hussars found some 'Oompah! Oompah!' instruments stored on the shores of Altersee, the lake in the centre of the devastated city. The Hussars dressed up as Nazis and gave a concert to some rather perplexed citizens. Not a man amongst them could play anything. The war in Germany was over.

NINETEEN

Elsewhere January-May 1945

The Gothic Line in Italy

The Allied objective in 1945 was to move from the Gothic Line, running from Pisa to Rimini, and move on north to Bologna and Milan. On 8 February, on 'The Pimple' near Florence, 'Corporal P.' of the Household Cavalry, famous for a previous incident, entered a personal crisis. He stood to attention on the trench parapet, clearly in a desperate state.

'Nerve has gone, sir,' he called out shakily to his company commander. 'Can I report to the M.O., sir?'

The captain stared at 'P.' keenly. He knew as well as anyone else in the regiment that 'P.'s' claim to fame was 'The Tale of the Horse with a Green Tail'. The story was that he had invited a young maiden round to his stable to see 'The Horse with the Green Tail'; she later complained that she was shown something completely different.

'Okay,' agreed the officer after much deliberation (should he let the bastard die?). 'Corporal P.' trudged off to the sound of some gentle whinnying and neighing from the trench.

Despite slow progress against the Gothic Line in February and March the troops continued to try and entertain themselves during rest periods. At the Teatre Nuo in Pischiello Captain C.R.S. Buckley of the Scots Guards put on the revue *Improperly Dressed*.

It was not to the liking of all the audience: indeed, some officers were outraged. James Agate of *The Sunday Times* decided that it was a 'revolting mixture of smut and sentiment'. Service personnel were advised to adjust their dress before leaving the theatre. Other ranks and some officers loved it, especially Captain Buckley's 'Solly the White Sultan', in which he performed 'snake-like writhing and gyrating'.

On the River Po, meanwhile, Christopher Thursby-Pelham and Joe Gurney preferred to go fishing. Their plan for this was to explode a bundle of gelignite sticks. They rowed out in a boat to the middle of the river but the wires touched the rudder and a premature explosion took place. Christopher and Joe were lucky to survive but had to swim for it surrounded by stunned fish. All-round, it was a loss-making day because they had to pay for the boat and it was the turn of their CO to let off a rocket.

Nearby, on 24 March, there was more entertainment in a local wood, where, it was rumoured, there was a 'nymph' offering certain services. The upshot of all this was that the whole guard was arrested for being absent from its post. However, the case against it was muddied by the large number of officers also present in the wood, though not on guard.

Philip Brutton was invited to dinner at a local palace and his eventual downfall centred around pre-dinner refreshment of Gordon's gin and Benevento gin, which was much like 'Hoochinoo' or 'Red Man's Revenge'. Philip was normally more than able to hold his drink but this lethal combination, combined with a touch of jaundice, caused him to career down an ancient corridor lined with suits of armour. It was an incredible feat of balance, in the circumstances, which enabled him to miss all these ancient warriors. If he had knocked one over the whole lot would have toppled like a line of dominoes. Valiant fellow troopers, Pritchard and Norris, piled him into a truck and safely back to bed.

The northern Italian cities fall

A more determined assault on the Gothic Line took place on 9 April. The Poles were in Bologna by the 21st and the New Zealanders passed through Mirabello on the 24th. Philip Brutton found them to be terrific chaps, if somewhat unscrupulous. One offered a German staff car for sale at 40,000 lire (about £100), took 20,000 from a customer and drove off at speed whilst the other 20,000 was being assembled. Italian partisans liberated Milan, and Turin went at the end of the month.

In Biella the already punch-drunk Germans suffered further bewilderment on 2 May when one of their armies surrendered to members of the Japanese-American Task Force. On the same day the President of Eire, Eamon de Valera, expressed his condolences on the death of Hitler to the German representative in Dublin.

The fall of Turin was an occasion for much celebration, even for Philip Brutton's batman, normally a man of the utmost sobriety. Bringing in dinner for his officer it took Private Jones a full two minutes to cross the room carrying out a superb piece of balancing, swaying violently from side to side and precariously juggling the mess tins, knees bent, eyes revolving. Brutton was quite hypnotised by this splendid dedication to duty.

Having slid the food onto the table Jones produced a low and dignified bow, burped, apologised in a slur, straightened up, about-turned and staggered back from whence he came. Brutton felt like applauding.

At home

Pam Ashford's colleagues in Glasgow continued to entertain. On 11 January Elaine, who was generally regarded as 'flighty', declared firmly that she did not fear starvation since she was attractive enough to land a rich husband at any time. But friends warned her that the amount of peroxide she used on her hair would cause it to fall out, ruining her chances of a profitable marriage. Elaine was of the opinion that this eventuality was long term and that she would be able to land her man before her hair fell out.

The winter was bitterly cold. Shop assistants in Glasgow wore gloves to serve; 26 January was particularly freezing and the BBC announced that the Minister of Fuel was asking people to cut down on the use of electricity. The request only produced loud and sustained ironic laughter in Pam's office.

On 31 January Pam and friends discussed Hitler's coming demise. There was some support for the forecast that he would retire, write his memoirs and live comfortably off the royalties for the remainder of his life. Another view was that he would vanish having had his face re-modelled by a top Nazi surgeon.

On 2 March the BBC also announced that more elastic would be made available for underwear. Already, many workers were off sick after suffering from draughts up the legs. Pam commented that any shyness about discussing knickers in public had long since gone. 'Knickers in brief', she pointed out, was a necessary public discourse.

V2s continued to spread alarm and despondency in London. In the week ending 15 February 180 people were killed. I couldn't believe it when, on 3 March, I spotted a V1 trundling over. We all thought they had finished. We hadn't seen one since September 1944. Perhaps it had got lost? I was suddenly petrified with fear because of this stray Doodlebug.

Lionel King, another boy a few miles away, had more cause to be alarmed: all the windows of his house in Leyton were blown out by a rocket.

'Cheer up, mate,' said the bloke mending them to Lionel's dad. 'Every time they fire one of those things off six Germans in the firing zone are killed.'

A War Reserve constable tried to move on a prostitute who was surrounded by GIs in the Edgware Road. She refused to budge. 'You're only a Utility copper,' she scoffed.

To try and make Lionel King and me feel better Bomber Command attacked a rocket site in the Hague, but missed and killed 520 Dutch. Next day it was the turn of the Americans, on Zurich, in neutral Switzerland: five Swiss died (on 22 February they had killed seventeen).

The other bad news was that U-boats could now stay indefinitely under water because the crew could breathe through something called a ''Schnorkel', and also that German airmen were flying in 'jet' planes. Adolf was not finished yet, so it seemed, although he told his advisers on 23 April that he was going to shoot himself as he assumed control of the defence of the city and sacked Goering. He not only sacked him but also sent out a warrant for his arrest. Two more conspirators were executed, all on the same day.

Japanese comedians, kamikaze and Joyce Grenfell

In the mopping-up operation in the Solomon Islands, west of New Guinea, Japanese guerrillas infiltrated Bougainville. Peter Pinney, an Australian, was setting clever traps for them. But the extra-special contraption he laid out on 6 January was actually removed by one of these Japanese, who substituted a 10-yen note.

'Who is the Jap with a sense of humour?' he wondered. 'How can you kill a bloke who makes you laugh?'

On 9 January the Americans landed at Luzon in the Philippines and were now confronted by kamikaze sailors in boats packed with explosives. In just ten days in January 625 American sailors were lost in this way. Lord Louis Mountbatten did come across a different type of Japanese warrior on 13 January. It was hard to capture one of them, anyway, but this one did not need persuasion or psychological treatment to induce him to divulge useful information. He gleefully offered to answer in detail any question the interrogators cared to try. In fact, he didn't need prompting at all as he informed them that he had recorded every incident of barbarity perpetrated on Allied POWs by the guards on the Bangkok–Thanbyuzuyat railway. He confessed that some of these beatings were inflicted for no apparent reason except that the prisoner's face offended the guard.

This officer explained that he was hoping to become 'an Honourable Member of the Honourable British Empire'. There were a few peculiar Japanese all over this war zone. George Wright-Nooth, a British prisoner held near Hong Kong, observed an American bombing raid on 16 January. One guard, who was known as 'The Schoolmaster', solemnly fixed his bayonet and clipped on ten rounds, kneeled down and pointed the weapon at the sky.

'You look plane,' he ordered George. 'When you see plane you say.' George spotted one at 20,000ft about 5 miles away and told The

Schoolmaster, who took careful aim and blazed away, confident that he was doing his duty.

First Lieutenant Sugihara Kinryu received a letter from his daughter during an American raid on Iwo Jima on 31 January:

Dear Father,

I am obeying mother and am studying hard to become a great lady. So please hurry and do away with Americans and return home to me.

General MacArthur led his army into Manila on 6 February. The Japanese homelands were now under threat. At dawn on 19 February marines landed on Iwo Jima. Sy Khan was elsewhere, having secured a day's leave in Dagupan in the Philippines. Sadly, it was not an enjoyable experience. There was no coffee anywhere and in the food shops hordes of flies covered the merchandise. Iwo Jima was captured on 26 March.

The US aircraft carrier Yorktown was off Okinawa on 26 March and the bakers down below were having a hard time. As soon as they put a cake in the oven it was the signal for the 5in guns to – in the words of Joe 'the baker' – 'start walking the dog'.

The dough was put in just right, the cake started to puff up and 'wham!' The cake fell flat on its face. It went in as a sponge and came out like a pancake. Or the sea suddenly swelled up and all the batter ran to one end of the pan. At one end the cake was soggy and burnt at the other.

'I sure wouldn't give that to a dogface,' declared Joe. 'Who called the Pacific "pacific", that's what I want to know?'

Not far away 2nd Lieutenant Fukozo Obara and his men were trying to dodge the Yorktown's shells down a foxhole. Two hours later they all emerged and each man's face was covered in a thick layer of soot. They slapped each other on the back laughing until the tears created canals down their happy faces. It was the Japanese version of 'Cheer up, mate!'

Joyce Grenfell was in Barrackpore near Calcutta on 25 January and was finding it difficult to perform because all the local crows and green parrots had gathered in nearby trees and were providing a loud background chorus. There were also low-flying aircraft overhead and noisy ox-carts and motorbikes on the adjacent road.

Moreover, an Indian in enormous black boots pushed past her as she was trying to sing and behind the transparent white ENSA screen a gardener watered the flowers but the shadows suggested he was doing something else. Only Joyce's comic genius saved the day.

Burma

In Rangoon prison camp Wing Commander Bill Hudson had only *toxa* to eat. *Toxa* was spinach. Happily, Bill acquired a taste for spinach. 'This is the pits,' he sighed in resignation. 'I'll be liking red-headed women next.' He waited for the Allied forces to free him and the Japanese defenders of the city were ordered to fight to the death but did a moonlight flit. All that Bill and the others heard was a truck driving off after dark. But they did find two letters from the guards:

Rangoon 29 April 1945,

Bravely you have come here opening prison gate. We have gone keeping your prisoner safely with Nipponese knightship. Afterwards we may meet again in the front somewhere. Then let us fight bravely each other. We had kept the gate's keys in the gate room,

Nipponese Army.

The second note read:

Rangoon, 29 April 1945

To the whole captured persons of Rangoon Jail. According to the Nippon military order, we hereby give you liberty and admit to leave this place at your own will. Regarding food and other materials kept in the compound, we give you permission to consume them, as far as your necessity is concerned.

We hope that we shall have an opportunity to meet you again at battlefield of somewhere.

We shall continue our war effort eternally in order to get the emancipation of all Asiatic Races.

Haruo Ito
Chief Officer of Rangoon Branch Jail.

Rangoon jail in May 1945. Messages from inmates to the RAF. (Reproduced by kind permission of the Trustees of the Imperial War Museum (IND4652))

Mandalay had been captured in March and Churchill announced: 'Thank God we have got a place whose name we can pronounce.' He had in mind the previous conquests of Meiktela, the Irrawaddy River and, especially, Pjawbwe – none of them household words in Britain.

With the war in Europe entering its final days, interest in General Slim's advance towards Rangoon intensified. For Slim, it was the last echo of Kipling's world.

'Some day,' he said to the 9th Battalion of the Borderers Regiment, mainly stalwarts from Cumbria, 'you'll be proud to say, "I was there".'

'We'd have to get out of the bloody place first,' pointed out 'Grandarse', one of Cumbria's best – not directly to the general, of course. They did have a mutual interest in Rangoon – that was 'where all the big boats' were. Slim had pulled off a great military trick with a decoy crossing of the Irrawaddy River, utterly confusing the enemy – as well as the 9th Borderers. They had to dig in at three different positions in three hours. Private Forster blamed Churchill, the royal family and Vera Lynn.

Slim's next move was to send advanced forces 80 miles behind enemy lines – Operation Character. At the sharp end of this was the 9th, surrounded by vastly larger enemy forces. Private Forster complained once more:

'In the shit again,' he roared. 'I've had it – me. We'll all get killed. F**k this!'

Private Nixon, usually at loggerheads with Forster, for once agreed. 'We'll be up to our goolies in water,' he claimed. 'Getting ate to bits by leeches and jungle sores whilst the little bastards'll be digging themselves in all the way to Rangoon. Rain? It'll just piss down forever. It'll be that deep in the paddy they'll have to take the Gurkhas out of the line or the poor little buggers'll drown.'

Forster changed tack to more immediate concerns. 'Who's smoking, eh?' He was the biggest fag-scrounger ever known to man.

'Bugger off, Forster, scrounge somewhere else,' suggested another pal.

'Ah, you miserable Egremont twat! Who's going to brew up, then? Eh, Wattie, you've got the tin.'

'Brew up, yourself,' retorted Wattie. 'I've carried the bloody thing all day.'

'Aw, wrap up, you miserable sod. Jock [this to Private George Macdonald Fraser, son of a Carlisle doctor and the author of *Quartered Safe out Here*, a superb testimony to these brave and comical soldiers, here translated from the Cumbrian], get the tin, lad.'

But Fraser also lacked enthusiasm for the job: it had been a backbreaking day.

'Aw, just get the bloody sticks, you idle Scotch git. You want us to strike the f***ing match, an' all? I could piss better char than your brew.'

But Grandarse had a much higher opinion of Fraser's tea. 'You brew a canny cup, Jock. You'll have to open a shop down Botcher Gate. You can have a sign outside – a Black Cat with its arse'ole wreathed in smiles.' (The Borderers were known as the Black Cats.)

The Church of Scotland canteen, still with the regiment, rescued them even though the Japanese were just up the road. The canteen consisted of two small ladies with a battered urn and a tray of currant buns.

'My goodness, Ennie,' exclaimed Mary. 'We're running out of sandwiches. And did I not say we need another tin of spam? Dearie me! More tea, boys?'

Having refreshed the 9th they rattled off in their battered and mud-encrusted truck. 'First gear, Ennie,' advised Mary, 'and don't rev the motor. Oh, my, take a hammer to it! Bye, bye, boys.' They inched forward, adjusting their hairpins.

'Up yours! Up yours! Up yours!' It was the 'Up yours' bird which was actually a large lizard with an unusual mating call.

'And up yours, too,' recited Jock Fraser.

With the enemy on all sides the Borderers had to be careful with security and had arranged a password – 'VICTORY'. If it was Monday it was 'V', Tuesday was 'I', Wednesday 'C', and so on.

But Grandarse had the problem of never knowing what day of the week it was. The sentries knew full well it was him standing in the gloom of the jungle; in fact, you would never mistake him for a Japanese soldier a mile away. But they insisted on the proper password.

'Aw, shit – aye, Victory,' he mumbled. 'Hang on, now. Hey, Wattie what day is it? Thursday? Already? Get away! Aye, well, let's see … Monday, Tuesday, Wednesday, Thursday … v … i … c – aye, that'll be right. Aye, Toch. I'm saying T for Toch. Are you there, Forster?'

'Alright, bollocks. Come in if your feet are clean,' relented Forster even though it was Friday.

Their sergeant was Hutton, also with the gift of the gab. 'They tell us you're a good cross-country runner,' he said to George Fraser, who couldn't deny this fact. 'And you're a first-class shot, an' all, aren't you? Good – you're just the man to be sniper-scout for the section.' This turned out to be the most dangerous job going – at the very front searching villages for the Japanese. If he saw one he'd have to fire a shot and then run for his life.

'So,' further reasoned Sergeant Hutton, 'he'd better be a good runner, hadn't he?'

'Does it matter?' replied George. 'I mean, if he's surrounded by bleedin' Japs he might as well be on crutches. Do I get danger money?'

'Extra pay?' exclaimed the sergeant in disbelief. 'Danger money? You greedy little git. It's right enough what they say about you Scotch, you're always on the scrounge.'

He was back the following day offering George extra fags and adding, 'Hey, Jock, are you any good at arithmetic?'

It turned out to be an exercise in counting the size of the British army, their division, their battalion and their section (Nine).

'Now,' declaimed Hutton, '17th Division is ahead of the 14th Army and this Battalion is leading the Division and Nine Section out in front, further south than any other bugger in South-East Asia Command – are you following this, Jock?'

'With interest, Sarn't Hutton. Do you know what a sadist is?'

'By, Jock, you're a lucky young fellow! The odds against being the leading man in the whole f***ing war effort against Japan is five million to one.'

Rangoon goes

The Japanese surrendered in the city in early May, and Nine Section, 9th Borderers, now discussed the prospects of a total Japanese capitulation. How resilient were they?

Nick was doubtful. 'When I see a f***ing Japani wallah crawling out of his f***ing hole with a white flag, I'll believe it then, not until.'

Grandarse was more optimistic. 'Mind you, Jap's been getting the shit knocked out of him over here and at Mandalay. He must have about had it, by this time.'

'Bollocks,' scoffed Nick. 'Them buggers have had it when they're dead. Look at that lot that committed hara-kiri in the hospital. Jap doesn't pack in, now and I'm telling you.'

'You f***ing pessimist. Spreading alarm and despondency! Christ, if griping would have won the war you would have it over after Dunkirk. You make me tired, Nixon!'

'Well, I'm not counting on him packing in,' interceded Forster. 'We'll have to chase the buggers all the way to Tokyo.'

'Bugger me!' exclaimed an exasperated Grandarse. 'Now, man, think on. Jap's been chased all the way down from Imphal, he's been beat here, he's been beat at Mandalay – bloody hell, you've more dead Japs on the road here than you've got hairs on your arse.'

'Not on your arse, though,' quipped Forster.

'Never mind my arse. What I'm saying is he must be marching on his chinstrap by now. And look here, Nick, supposing you were a Jap ...'

'Ah, so! Me Jap, me sit in bunker, wait for Grandarse, stick bayonet up honnelable jacksy ...'

'If you were a Jap,' persevered Grandarse, 'and saw this lot coming – Gurkhas and Pathans, and Sikhs, and them bloody great black buggers from the East African Division, f***ing Zulus or something, and us, wouldn't you pack it in? I'm bloody sure he would. Well, Jap isn't bloody stupid.'

'Of course he's stupid,' insisted Nixon. 'He commits suicide, doesn't he. That's as stupid as you can get.'

'Aye, but there's a limit,' concluded Grandarse. 'That's what I'm saying, see. He's bound to pack it in sometime!'

There were actually fears that cut-off Japanese soldiers would mingle with other South-East Asians and you wouldn't be able to tell the difference. But there was a theory that you could tell if he was Japanese by the way he ate a banana – cutting it in half and squeezing out each half. Moreover, a further test was that a Japanese big toe was well separated from the rest of their toes. Sadly, diligent research found that Koreans also had funny big toes.

TWENTY

VE and VJ Day

Getting ready

American POWs near Berlin prepared for liberation. The last guard left at Red Prendergast's camp had a wooden leg. But even he cleared off when the news of the Führer's death filtered through. Red and comrades then rushed madly for the American lines: sadly, they couldn't find them. They were no luckier with the Russians. They tore madly through Meissen six times looking for any Allied soldier – anyone, whilst eating all the local seed potatoes being saved for 1946.

On the eve of VE Day they slept in a deserted apartment block. But in the dead of night Red was awakened by someone creeping into his room with a dim flashlight.

'Vas vants you?' snarled Red pointing a pistol at the moving shadow.

'Mein teddy bear,' answered a tiny voice.

The big day – 8 May 1945

Kenneth Richmond, a Mass Observationist, travelled to work very early on 8 May and the first celebratory flag he spotted was one about 3in square on top of a very tall flag pole. Homemade efforts were the order of the day, as seen in the picture.

Things heated up later in the day and it was a great night out in the West End. A snake-like procession of girls and GIs weaved along Charing Cross Road carrying a naked man shoulder-high, he was crowned in silver leaves and waving a chamber pot. There was another one on top of the statue of Eros in Piccadilly Circus – a sailor, by all accounts. Princesses Elizabeth and Margaret slipped unnoticed into Trafalgar Square and did not get back to the palace until the early hours. A friend of Richmond's said hopefully: 'Perhaps Phyllis Dixie will have too much to drink tonight and drop her fan.'

Humphrey Lyttleton, the famous jazz musician, was outside Buckingham Palace playing his trumpet and was joined by a bloke with a drum strapped to his chest, a trombonist and someone with an enormous horn. They led a vast parade to Trafalgar Square with Lyttleton being pushed along in a handcart.

There was celebration in Germany, too. The signaller of the 3rd Battalion of the Royal Horse Artillery (RHA), at Itzehoe, near the Kiel Canal, fell out of a window and broke his arm. He had survived North Africa and Normandy. Fellow RHA liberated the wine reserve at the Hamburg Amerika Steamship Company.

It was a tumultuous few days. By the 11th Kenneth Richmond was, in his own words, 'bewitched, buggered and bewildered', whilst my father fell off a bus on the Isle of Dogs after also liberating booze from the Millwall Docks.

Getting out the flags on VE Day. (Reproduced by kind permission of the Trustees of the Imperial War Museum (49414))

CHEER UP, MATE!

Meanwhile, Peter Ota, an American Japanese, waited anxiously in Southampton with his comrades whilst Command pondered over whether to send them to Okinawa, where they might be mistaken for real Japanese.

Praise continued to be heaped on Winston Churchill, our great war leader:

> One sniff of the Old Havana,
> We'd follow him right to Fugi – Yama.
> We'd follow him most anywhere,
> The man with the big cigar.

Near the end of July Labour won the General Election with a landslide victory. Thanks, Winnie, now clear off.

VJ Day

Someone said to Bill Bailey of the US Navy: 'An Adam Bomb has destroyed a whole Japanese city.'

'This son-of-a-bitch Adam – who the hell is he?' wondered Bill.

Nine Section of the 9th Borderers had their own debates:

'Hey, Grandarse, hear what they're saying on the wireless?' reported Nick. 'The Yanks have dropped a bomb the size of a pencil on Tokyo and it's blown the whole f***ing place to bits.'

'Oh, aye, what were they aiming at – Hong Kong,' scoffed Grandarse.

'I'm telling you. Just one little bomb and they reckon half of Japan's in f***ing flames. They reckon Jap'll pack it in.'

But Grandarse had altered his view of Japanese durability. 'Get away! Do them yellow-skined buggers out there know?' He was referring to the fact that there were still plenty of them in Burma.

'Aw, bloody hell! How can they, you daft bugger. They haven't got the f***ing wireless, have they?'

'Alright, then but I'm keeping my head down until the Yanks have dropped a few more pencils on Tokyo.'

The Andrews Sisters were doing a show in Naples on 15 August but the audience of 8,000 American troops were not happy. They were waiting to be embarked for the Pacific. A note was passed on stage and Patty read it out aloud without reading it to herself first. In this way she announced the end of the war. Everybody on stage started crying whilst the audience was dumbstruck.

This lasted a few seconds, and then all hell let loose – shirts, even trousers, were flung high into the air and one guy fell off the rafters. Patty met him in a lift in Cleveland thirty years later.

Muriel Green, the Mass Observationist, wrote in her diary: 'A new people's Parliament has opened and the world is ready for better things.'

Nella Last, a fellow diarist, took two aspirins and tried to read herself to sleep.

Bibliography

Aldridge, Richard J., *Witness to War*, London, 2004
———, *The Faraway War*, London, 2005
Ardizzone, Edward, *Diary of a War Artist*, London, 1974
Arthur, Max, *Lost Voices of the Royal Air Force*, London, 2005
———, *Lost Voices of the Royal Navy*, London, 2005
———, *Last of the Few*, London, 2010
Bailey, Roderick, *Forgotten Voices of D-Day*, London, 2009
Beardmore, George, *Civilian at War*, Oxford, 1986
Binns, Stewart, Carter, Lucy and Wood, Adrian, *Britain at War in Colour*, London, 2000
Bishop, Patrick, *Fighter Boys*, London, 2004
———, *Bomber Boys*, London, 2007
Bowlby, Alex, *The Recollections of Rifleman Bowlby*, London, 1969
Brown, Mike and Harris, Carol *The Wartime House: Home Life in Wartime Britain*, Stroud, 2001
Brutton, Philip, *Ensign in Italy*, London, 1992
Bryant, Mark, *World War II in Cartoons*, Swindon, 1989
Burgett, Donald, *Beyond the Rhine*, Novata, California, 2001
Calder, Angus, *The People's War: Britain 1939–45*, London, 1969
Campbell Begg, Richard and Liddle, Peter H., *Experiencing war 1939–45*, London, 2002
Carroll, David, *The Home Guard*, Stroud, 1999
Clay, Catrine, *Trautmann's Journey: from Hitler Youth to FA Cup Legend*, London, 2010
Cowper, Marcus, *The Words of War*, Edinburgh, 2009

Crimp, R.L., *The Diary of a Desert Rat*, London, 1971

Croall, Jonathan, *Don't You Know There's a War On? The People's Voice*, London, 1988

Crook, D.M., *Spitfire Pilot: A Personal Account of the Battle of Britain*, London, 2008

Currie, Jack, *Lancaster Target*, Oxford, 2006

Davies, Ron, *One Man's War*, Stroud, 2008

Dezarrois, André (translated by Stead, P.J.), *The Mouchotte Diaries*, Bristol, 2004

Delaforce, Patrick, *Churchill's Desert Rats in North Africa, Sicily and Italy*, Barnsley, 2009

———, *Churchill's Desert Rats in North-West Europe*, Barnsley, 2010

Fraser, George Macdonald, *Quartered Safe Out Here*, London, 1992

Ford, Ken, *Mailed Fist. 6th Armoured Division at War 1940–45*, Stroud, 2005

Fountain, Nigel (ed.), *World War II: The People's Story*, London, 2003

Fowler, William, *We Gave Our Today: Burma 1941–45*, London, 2009

Gardiner, Juliet, *Over Here: The GIs in Wartime Britain*, London, 1992

———, *Wartime Britain 1939–1945*, London, 2004

———, *The Children's War*, London, 2005

———, *The Blitz. The British Under Attack*, London, 2010

Garfield, Simon, *Private Battles*, London, 2002

———, *We are at War*, London, 2005

Gilbert, Martin, *The Second World War: A Complete History*, London, 2009

Grant, Ian and Maddren, Nicholas: *The Countryside at War*, London, 1975

Grenfell, Joyce, *The Time of My Life: Entertaining the Troops*, Oxford, 1990

Holland, James, *Twenty One: Coming of Age in the Second World War*, London, 2006

Koa Wing, Sandra: *Our Longest Days: A People's History of the Second World War*, London, 2008

Kershaw, Robert: *Never Surrender: Lost Voices of a Generation at War*, London, 2009

Kramer, Ann, *Land Girls and their Impact*, Barnsley, 2008

Last, Nella, *Nella Last's War: The Second World War Diaries of a Housewife*, London, 2006

BIBLIOGRAPHY

Lewis, Jon (ed.), *D-Day As They Saw it*, London, 2004

———, *World War II: The Autobiography*, London, 2009

Levine, Joshua, *Forgotten Voices of the Blitz & the Battle for Britain*, London, 2007

———, *Forgotten Voices of Dunkirk*, London, 2010

Lowry, Michael, *Fighting Through to Kohima*, Barnsley, 2003

Macintyre, Ben, *Operation Mincemeat*, London, 2010

Mack, Joanna and Humphries, Steve, *The Making of Modern London*, London, 1985

Millgate, Helen D., *Mr. Brown's War: A Diary of the Second World War*, Stroud, 1998

———, *Got Any Gum, Chum?*, Stroud, 2009

Milligan, Spike, *Adolf Hitler: My Part in His Downfall*, London, 1972

———, *Monty: His Part in My Downfall*, London, 1978

Moorehead, Alan, *African Trilogy*, London, 1965

Morris, Monica B., *Goodnight Children Everywhere*, Stroud, 2009

Moynihan, Michael, *People at War 1939–1945*, London, 1974

Parkhouse, Hardy, *Diary of a Soldier*, Durham, 1993

Parsons, Martin, *Waiting to Go Home*, Denton, 1999

Perrault, Giles (translated by Ortzen, Len), *The Secrets of D-Day*, London, 1964

Rohmer, Richard, *Patton's Gap: An Account of the Battle of Normandy*, London, 1981

Rolfe, Mel, *Hell on Earth*, London, 1999

Sarkar, Dilip, *Last of the Few*, Stroud, 2010

Shaw, Frank & Shaw, Joan, *We Remember Dunkirk*, Oxford, 1997

Sheridan, Dorothy (ed.), *Wartime Women*, London, 2000

Stansky, Peter, *The First Day of the Blitz*, New Haven & London, 2007

Steinbeck, John, *Once There Was a War*, London, 1994

Terkel, Studs, *The Good War: An American Oral History of World War II*, London, 1984

Thomas, Donald, *An Underworld at War*, London, 2004

Thompson, Julian, *Forgotten Voices of Burma*, London, 2010

Wheal, Donald James, *World's End*, London, 2005

INDEX

INDEX

Other titles published by The History Press

Don't You Know There's a War On?
Jonathan Croall
£8.09

Gathering together the personal stories of thirty-five people, drawn from all walks of life, this book evokes the reality of life in Britain during the Second World War. Here is a personal portrait of a nation at war, with contemporary photographs, diaries, letters, poems, and other memorabilia belonging to the men and women whose wartime lives are featured.

978-0-7509-3699-6

Bagels & Bacon: The Postwar East End
Jeff Rozelaar
£11.69

Jeff Rozelaar was born into a Jewish family and raised in the East End. A lucky survivor of the Nazi menace, he played in the streets among the debris with his schoolmates. This vivid account of growing up is told with passion and humour. The captivating anecdotes within, both poignant and entertaining, are immersed in the sights, sounds and smells of the East End in the post-war era.

978-0-7524-5870-0

A Bloody Picnic: Tommy's Humour, 1914–18
Alan Weeks
£8.99

One of the crucial factors that kept Tommy going on the Western Front was his ability to see what was comic in the horror, deprivation and discomfort of trench warfare. Providing the same level of amusement now as it did then, *A Bloody Picnic* presents an unusual perspective on how soldiers coped with the grim realities of the First World War.

978-0-7524-5668-3

Tea, Rum & Fags
Alan Weeks
£11.69

It is said that 'an army marches on its stomach,' but histories of the First World War usually overlook this and concentrate on its political and military aspects. From a civilised supper of beer, wine, egg and chips in a town, to making do with bully beef in a water-filled trench the next day, Alan Weeks examines how the army got its food and drink and what it was like.

978-0-7524-5000-1

Visit our website and discover thousands of other History Press books.

www.thehistorypress.co.uk